Bubblin' Over

Simple Ideas for Spectacular Parties

Ann Cain
Melisa Buchanan

© 1991 *by*
Oak Plantation Press
Rockwall, Texas 75087

Publisher's Cataloging in Publication
(Prepared by Quality Books Inc.)

Cain, Ann, 1952-
  Bubblin' over--simple ideas for spectacular parties / Ann Cain, Melisa Buchanan.--
  p. cm.
  ISBN 1-879129-01-9

  1. Entertaining. 2. Dinners and dining. I. Buchanan, Melisa, 1951- II. Title.

TX731   793.2
                                        QBI91-167

OAK PLANTATION PRESS

P.O. Box 640   Rockwall, Texas 75087-0640

914923

Acknowledgements

Thank you Dewayne, Amy and Chris for your love and encouragement. The love and laughter we share every day is better than any party in the world!

A.C.

To Barry, Matthew, Mindy and Beth--thanks for supporting me with your enthusiam and your laughter.

M.B.

Introduction

Spectacular parties do *not* require gourmet cooks, hundreds of dollars, or long hours of preparation. However, they *do* require imagination, enthusiasm and careful planning. In fact, the best party of all is one that makes its guests feel comfortable and special!

As two active women, we find our daily roles often frustrating and draining: wives, mothers, volunteers, carpoolers, committee chairmen, and businesswomen, too. The very thought of gathering our friends for a party ignites our creative minds and souls. Together, we have shared countless happy hours of planning and hosting these and other parties.

We hope that this book will be the spark you need to bring your love for entertaining to a full flame. The ideas included are adaptable to your own home, budget, guest list, and entertaining style. Like stoking a fire, use your individuality to fuel our ideas. You will soon be . . . *Bubblin' Over,* too!

A Word of Explanation

Bubblin'Over - Simple Ideas for Spectacular Parties is a versatile guide to creative party planning. Hundreds of unique suggestions are presented as invitations, mood sets, entertainment, mementoes and menus.

For your convenience, some recipes from each party have been included at the back of the book. They are noted in the suggested menu with an asterisk. These recipes are family favorites or have been shared by treasured friends and are sure to please.

As you read the book, select those ideas that fit your party needs. You will discover that most of the ideas are adaptable and interchangeable. For example, the "Two By Two" costume party can also be a delightful Halloween party. The "Gone With the Wind" birthday party can double as a grand anniversary celebration.

You may choose to use only some of the suggestions for each party. You may wish to combine the ideas from two different parties. Take the ideas, embellish them, adapt them, but most importantly - enjoy them. You will soon be *Bubblin' Over,* too!

About the Authors

Ann Cain is a graduate of Southern Methodist University. A former elementary school teacher, she is now actively involved in the family business, is an enthusiastic volunteer for various school and civic organizations, and devotes many enjoyable hours to her church. Childhood memories of family gatherings, and special occasion parties contribute to her love of entertaining. She is married, and has two wonderful children.

Melisa Buchanan, a graduate of the University of North Texas, is a former teacher and educational consultant. She is the author of *Teach a Beginning Reader with Common Sense and a Cookie Sheet*. Active in school, community and church groups, she is married and is the mother of three busy children.

About the Illustrator

Lynn Etta Manning is a graduate of Southern Methodist University and presently is owner of The Lion's Pen, an art design studio. As with the two authors, she is busy with many philanthropic and church activities in her community. She is married and has two children.

The two authors and the illustrator are friends who share an interest in entertaining. All three are native Texans who now live in the Dallas-Ft. Worth area.

Contents

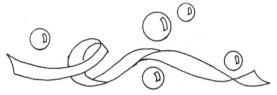

Gather in the Garden   1

Gardening gloves, tools and colorful seed packets help create the mood for this ''fresh from the garden'' buffet party.

Caribbean Caper   5

You will create your own tropical island for this buffet party.

Grubs and Shrubs Housewarming   9

When guests appear with shrubs and shovels in hand, the fun begins.

Spring Fling   13

A novel backyard barbecue full of bounce!

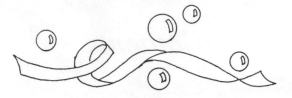

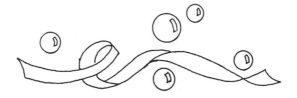

Be True to Your School   45

"Rah! Rah! for the old team" when each guest arrives as the mascot of his alma mater.

Comfy Cozy Quilt Party   49

Treasured family quilts provide the inspiration for this intimate gathering of friends.

Cookie House Brunch   53

Friends, young and old, gather for holiday brunch and leave with a spectacular memento.

Wine Down   57

Relax with friends after the rush of the holidays with this simple party solution.

A Gilded Gala   59

Celebrate old friendships and cultivate new ones during this elegant dinner party.

Dinner with the Captain   63

On your luxury cruise liner, every guest will double as a member of the Captain's crew.

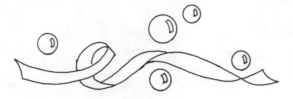

Purple Passion Party 99

Loads of "purple" fun make this youthful birthday celebration one to remember.

Keep This Under Your Hat 103

Careful planning and clever friends ensure the success of this individualized surprise party.

Flamin' Forties Frolic 107

Try this "Red Hot" revelry for the next 40th birthday celebration.

Gone With The Wind 111

This lavish birthday party is a superb way to celebrate the passing of youth.

Something Old, Something New 115

Any bride will adore gifts which blend the past with the present.

It's In The Bag 119

Food, flowers, frivolity, everything for this delightful bridal shower is in the bag.

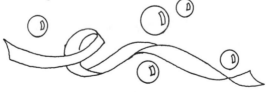

Recipes 125

Gather in the Garden

Even if you are not a superb gardener, late spring and early summer provide a bounty of home-grown vegetables and fruits. No one will be able to resist the flavors of a "fresh-from-the-garden" meal.

INVITATION:
Select colorful gardening gloves to hold your invitations. Then, write the invitations on bright notecards and tuck one inside a glove for each guest. The invitations can be mailed or delivered in person.

The garden was planted
We watched it grow
The riches of harvest
Now we can show!
Come for dinner from the garden!
June 30th   6:30 p.m.
The Cain's Garden

MOOD SET:

If you have your own vegetable garden or fruit orchard, what better setting for cocktails and appetizers? If not, set a garden mood outside or inside, using rakes, shovels, hoes, watering cans, baskets and clay pots filled with plants, vegetables and fruit. Use a wheelbarrow to ice canned drinks and a new metal garden pail as an ice bucket. A small garden spade serves as the ice scoop to fill glasses for iced tea or lemonade. For an attractive appetizer, hollow a head of purple cabbage and fill it with vegetable dip. Place this on a tray and surround it with fresh, raw vegetables.

Check fabric stores for a fruit or vegetable print fabric to use for making a tablecloth, napkins and a bibbed apron for the gourmet garden chef. A large produce or gathering basket overflowing with colorful vegetables and topped with a perky bow is a simple but appropriate centerpiece. A collection of gardening necessities, such as gloves, bright seed packets and small garden tools might surround the basket. Individual zinnia plants and

2

garden tools complete the tablescape and may serve as both placecards and mementoes for your guests. Consider serving one or more of your menu items from large terra cotta clay pots, wicker baskets or garden pails.

ENTERTAINMENT:

As dessert is served, provide pens and paper to each guest with the instructions to complete the following questionnaire. Collect the responses and read them aloud one at a time. Guests must guess whose answers are whose. Sample questions:

1. Describe yourself as a fruit and explain why that fruit best represents you.
2. Describe yourself as a vegetable and explain why that vegetable best represents you.
3. Describe the person seated to your right as a fruit or vegetable and explain why.
4. Name the vegetable you most despised as a child and describe any tricks you used to avoid eating it.

MENU:

Okra Gumbo*
Summer Squash Casserole
Corn on the Cob
Fresh Green Beans
Black-eyed Peas
New Potatoes
Sliced Tomatoes
Pickled Beets*
Green Tomato Relish*
Corn Bread
Hot Peach Cobbler with Fresh Cream

MEMENTO:

Any small bedding plant that is in bloom makes a colorful and appropriate gift. Wrap the plastic plant containers with scraps of fabric left from the tablecloth and secure with colorful ribbon bows. Small garden tools or gardening books also make welcomed mementoes.

Caribbean Caper

Hear the calypso beat? Feel the balmy ocean breeze? This party promises to fill the night with the sights, sounds and smells of a Caribbean paradise.

INVITATION:

Write your invitation on hot pink notecards or on notecards printed with a flamingo or beach scene. Tuck the invitations into large conch shells. Often you can buy these inexpensive shells at a craft or import store. Disguise your shell invitations in fluffy hot pink or turquoise tissue paper and place them in hot pink or turquoise gift bags. Personally deliver your invitations to the guests.

A tropical beach
with setting sun,
Sparkling water,
Caribbean fun.
Casual dress, a Calypso sound
Come at 7, we're island bound.
Buffet supper on the 10th of June
Join us 'neath a Caribbean moon.

The Carters   710 Bayview   R.S.V.P.

MOOD SET:

A flock of pink flamingos will set the stage for this Caribbean Caper. Standing 2 to 3 feet high, these flamingos can easily be made from plywood and dowel rods. After they are painted hot pink, your flamingos will provide a whimsical focal point. Create a lush background of foliage by grouping your household tropical plants and ferns; you can easily borrow your friends' plants to use as well. Other festive touches might include  pieces of wicker furniture, bird cages, bright tropical flowers, a hammock, snorkels, flippers, masks, strawbags or even mounted trophy fish.

You may want to use lawn torches to provide both effective lighting and an enchanting atmosphere. Lawn torches can often be purchased at import or swimming pool supply stores.

Make additional lights by punching a pattern of holes in empty coffee cans. Spray paint the cans hot pink or turquoise. Place approximately 2 inches of sand in each can and set a votive candle inside.

6

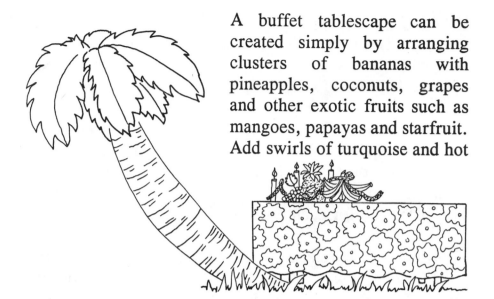

A buffet tablescape can be created simply by arranging clusters of bananas with pineapples, coconuts, grapes and other exotic fruits such as mangoes, papayas and starfruit. Add swirls of turquoise and hot pink curling ribbon intertwined through the fruit and additional sea shells. Choose bright tropical-print napkins, or you could easily make your own. Search your craft or import stores for a fun "Caribbean souvenir" to use as a napkin decoration.

Plain white plates will look attractive with the addition of a single fresh flower, perhaps a vanda orchid. Or, you may choose to cover each plate with a palm frond before arranging the food.

For an amusing touch, ice canned beverages or wine bottles in a sailboat. A small boat is easy to set up and gives simple access to the beverages.

Most importantly, provide recordings of lively calypso music in the background. Your guests will frolic to the rhythm of the Caribbean.

ENTERTAINMENT:

Barefoot Treasure - Fill a child's inflatable swimming pool with clean sand. Let your guests search for buried silver dollars using only their feet.

Lunatic Limbo - Even the sanest of adults will enjoy a round of limbo. While a rod or stick is suspended between two braces, each person can try to go under the horizontal rod without falling or touching the ground. Lower the rod for each round until a winner is declared.

Fabric Folly - Purchase yards of inexpensive fabric with bright, bold flowers. Give each guest 1 to 2 yards of fabric. Provide scissors and safety pins, and have your guests create a Caribbean fashion: a scarf, waist wrap, hat or any imaginative item.

MENU:
 Fresh Chilled Shrimp or Crab Claw Cocktail
 Grilled Center Cut of Ham
 Curry Sauce*
 Perky Pineapple*
 Raspberry Parfait*
 Jamaican Blue Mountain Coffee

MEMENTO:
The ''Caribbean souvenir'' purchased to use as a napkin decoration will make an ideal memento.

When friends face the task of landscaping a new home, you can host a very special kind of housewarming. From a master landscaping plan designed for your friends' home, assign each guest a specific shrub to bring to the housewarming. The result is an overwhelmingly popular party *plus* instant landscaping for your friends.

INVITATION:

For distinctive invitations, use a pen and ink drawing of the new home and then write a poem of invitation. Duplicate copies, tri-fold, and mail to guests.

Ken & Rose are such nice guys,
But landscaping chores they do despise!
And since their yard is quite brand new,
We thought we'd ask some help from you.
So anytime from 4 to 9
On Sunday, May 1st ~ rain or shine,
We'll supply the food and fun.
But would you bring a shrub, just one?
Be very certain to wear your grubs...
We're really going to plant the shrubs!

The Tates' new address is 16 Josey Ln.
in Rockwall
Hosts: Mark & Becky Elliston
Barry & Missy Buchanan
If you would like to join in the fun of this
"Grubs & Shrubs" party, please bring a one-gallon...

MOOD SET:

Since this party is geared for the outside, the mood set should be simple and light-hearted. After all, your guests will be arriving in their "grubby" clothes.

Decorations and a snack buffet tablescape should reflect the spirit of this playful party. An arrangement of fresh-cut flowers in a watering can will serve as centerpiece. Arrange gardening gloves, hand tools, watering hoses or sprinklers, bedding plants and packages of seeds to complete your tablescape on a green-draped buffet table.

Since this is only a snack buffet, small disposable plates are in order. You might choose green plastic plates complemented by pretty floral napkins or paper napkins imprinted with the new homeowners' name.

Also, round up a selection of shovels, hoes, rakes, etc. to add to the atmosphere and to use for planting the shrubs. A wheelbarrow can become a cooler for icing beverages. Chips, pretzels and other finger foods can be served in terra cotta pots lined with coordinating napkins.

MOOD SET:

Of course, the primary purpose of this party is to welcome the friends to a new home while aiding them in their landscape efforts. Before this party can be successful, a certain amount of advance planning and work is required. Hopefully, the new homeowners can provide you with a master landscape plan which specifies shrub type, quantity and placement. The bedding areas must be prepared before the party (tilled, mulched, etc.) according to the plan.

Using the master landscape plan, determine the type of shrub you will write on each person's invitation. For example, if the plan requires 15 dwarf yaupon holly shrubs and 10 dwarf Chinese holly shrubs, then designate accordingly for 25 guests. Make labels out of poster board to mark the place for each shrub so that when guests arrive they will be able to find the location for their particular plants. Be sure to provide root stimulator for the newly-planted shrubs. As the guests complete their planting tasks, they will be ready for cool drinks and snacks. Lawn chairs, hammocks, and even quilts will be inviting. The new homeowners are free to mingle and enjoy their guests while their lawn becomes more attractive.

ENTERTAINMENT:

Since this party is designed as a come-and-go affair, you will probably have a steady stream of people. Therefore, the main activity is planting shrubs and no other entertainment is required.

MENU:

Assorted Chips and Crackers
Grub-And-Shrub Subs
Sliced Veggies and Digger's Dip*
Lemonade or Canned Beverages

MEMENTO:

A package of seeds will make a great memento for this special housewarming party.

Spring Fling

The first backyard barbecue of the season is sure to put a "spring" in the steps of your friends. Your local hardware store is the source for a novel idea sure to make this a party full of bounce.

INVITATION:

An every day coil spring, available at any hardware store, will become the vase for each spring blossom invitation. Spray paint each spring and insert a fresh or silk blossom. Inscribe color-coordinated cards with party details and attach with ribbon to the springs. Either deliver the invitation by hand or mail in a mailing tube.

Bounce by
for Burgers
March 7   8 P.M.
The Mannings

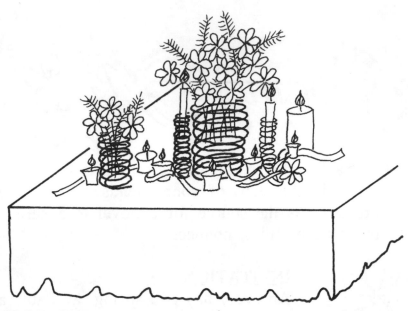

MOOD SET:

Set an informal mood with your favorite light-hearted music. Planters and baskets of spring blossoms should be abundant. Purchase an assortment of springs appropriate in sizes for holding small bouquets. Prepare a novel tablescape by grouping the unique "spring" vases with an assortment of candles that fit safely into the springs. For additional color, randomly tie a few candles and vases with ribbon bows.

Select your choice of linens, paper goods and dinnerware to carry out the color scheme. Roll silverware inside each napkin, securing with a small spring and top with a matching bow.

ENTERTAINMENT:

"Spring Fling" is a simple social that is suitable for any group or age; plan activities and/or games accordingly.

If room allows, teens, adults and children enjoy a friendly game of volleyball or softball. Provide kites for those who might enjoy a less physical activity.

MENU:

Grilled Hamburgers
Your Favorite Condiments and Relishes
Mother's Baked Beans*
Potato Salad
Assorted Cookies
Fruit and Cheese Tray
Lemonade or Soft Drinks

MEMENTO:

If you are entertaining adults, present each couple with a new, long-handled barbecue spatula. These are often available in bright colors and can be accented with a matching bow for a fun and inexpensive memento. Teens and children will enjoy a kite for catching the spring breezes.

15

Pastel Picnic

A palette of luscious, pastel colors and a picnic basket filled with tempting tidbits make a wonderful combination to enjoy with friends in a casual celebration of the springtime season.

INVITATION:
An artist's sketch pad with party information written in pastels is a perfect introduction. Be sure to spray the invitations with a sealer before enclosing in the envelope.

A tisket, a tasket,
A pastel picnic basket.
Luscious colors & candlelight.
A basket for two,
We hope will delight.
May 16 7:00 p.m.
The Stewarts

MOOD SET:

Lovely old quilts or pastel cloths used as table coverings or for lawn seating provide the perfect "pastel palette." Your baskets for two may be lined with a pastel plaid or print fabric. If you aren't too handy with a needle and thread, use pinking shears to finish any unhemmed fabric edges. With each couple's basket you might want to include the makings for their own intimate tablescape: a votive candle with holder, matches, fresh flowers, a bud vase, pastel ribbon, tissue paper, etc. Guests will enjoy comparing their creations. Dining indoors or outdoors, your entertainment area should abound with baskets of flowering plants. For a celestial touch, string twinkling white lights through live trees if you are dining outdoors, or through a grouping of silk trees and plants if your picnic is indoors. Easy listening music should play in the background.

ENTERTAINMENT:

Contact your local high school or college art department or area art guild for someone you can hire to do pastel sketching. Guests will enjoy watching an artist at work during cocktails. The finished product(s) might be presented to a lucky guest.

MENU:

You will need baskets large enough to accommodate servings for two. Be sure to include plates, napkins, silverware and wine glasses.

Vermicelli Salad*
Grilled Chicken Fillet Sandwich
Apricot Squares*
Bottle of White Wine

<u>MEMENTO</u>:
Present a box of pastels to each couple, with instructions to encourage their artistic endeavors.

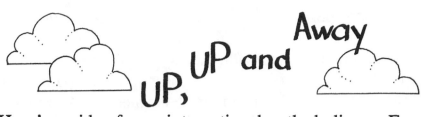

UP, UP and Away

Here's an idea for an international potluck dinner. From the moment your hot air balloon invitations are delivered, your guests will be anxious to attend.

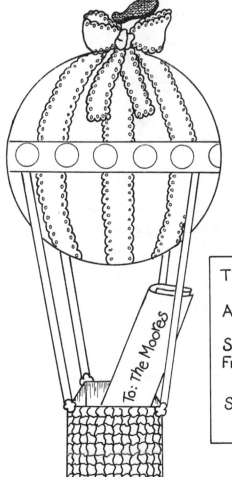

To: The Moores

INVITATION:

A miniature hot air balloon fashioned from a 3-inch diameter foam ball is a snap to make. Cover the foam ball with colored tulle netting that has been cut into a circle slightly larger than the ball. Gather the netting tightly around the ball and tie with a narrow coordina-

This hot air balloon has arrived
To take you for a special ride.
Any place you'd like to go
Tahiti, France, or Mexico?
Surprise us with your favorite dish
From your favorite land, your dream,
your wish!

Saturday, June 12   The Flints
7:00 p.m.   700 Chicago

21

ting ribbon, permitting any excess ribbon to dangle from the bow. Next, glue metallic trim around the center. Then be creative with other decorations: ribbon, lace, sequins, etc. Attach four round lollipop sticks painted in a matching color. (You can purchase these sticks at most craft stores.) Glue a miniature basket to the sticks.

Put a copy of the poem/invitation inside each basket, and your hot air balloon is complete. Deliver the invitations by hand. If you choose not to make the hot air balloons, consider purchasing stationery or postcards with a hot air balloon motif.

MOOD SET:
Since each guest's fantasy destination will be a surprise, you can set the party mood with world-wide travel apparatus: luggage, travel brochures, maps and souvenirs from anywhere! Combine hula skirts, sombreros, seashells and such with any travel memorabilia: passports, postcards, photographs and foreign money. A travel agency is a great source for posters and travel brochures, particularly if they are a bit out-dated.

A large hot air balloon can easily become an effective centerpiece. Follow the directions for making the smaller hot air balloon invitations, substituting a 12-inch ball and using dowel rods rather than lollipop sticks. Fill the basket with more travel guides, maps, a camera and film allowing colorful ribbon to overflow the basket's rim.

This potluck dinner will be served as a casual buffet. Be prepared with serving spoons and forks, and have plenty of refrigerator or oven space for guests' dishes until dinner is ready to be served.

ENTERTAINMENT:
The fun of this party is listening to the many fantasy destinations and eating the international cuisine. Also, consider creating your own Geography Trivia contest with questions about foreign customs, monetary names, tourist locations, etc.

MENU:
The food will be provided by your guests, but be prepared with a selection of breads and beverages to complete the meal.

MEMENTO:
A personalized luggage tag for each guest will be a useful memento of this party.

Shine On Harvest Moon

The rich, full bounty of harvest time brings a glorious array of colorful leaves, fruits and vegetables. Traditionally, the harvest moon is said to shine so brightly that farmers can work until late at night to bring in their crops. With a little advance planning your fall feast will be set aglow. . . . Shine on, Harvest Moon.

INVITATION:

First, check your calendar for dates of a full moon during early fall. Purchase simple white invitations of nice quality paper, or make your own by cutting "full moon" circles from white art board. Using gold ink inscribe the following message on each invitation:

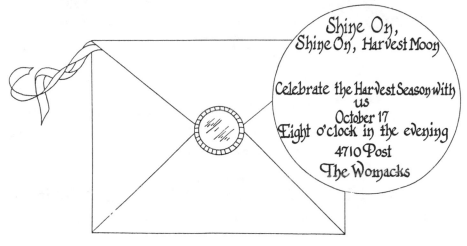

Address white envelopes with matching gold ink. Be sure to include a few strips of gold tinsel (Christmas variety) so that "moon beams" spill from the envelope when opened.

MOOD SET:
A magnificent full moon speaks for itself! Weather permitting, serve cocktails outdoors on a porch or in a gazebo so that your guests will be bathed in lustrous moonglow. Inside, candles should be plentiful so that a soft, warm glow spreads throughout the entertainment area.

Exposing the natural wood grain of the dining table will lend a rich feeling. Begin the tablescape with brass candlesticks of all shapes and sizes topped with cream-colored candles. Add other decorative brass objects to this grouping and complete the tablescape with small pumpkins, apples, squash, etc. Small shafts of wheat, baskets of golden yellow, rust or deep red chrysanthemum plants and/or clusters of fall leaves will combine nicely. To protect the table top, loosely center a yard or two of soft, cream-colored fabric on the table and position the decorations along the fabric.

Choose rich, plaid placemats, coordinating napkins in vibrant fall colors and a simple dinnerware pattern.

26

For placecards, bundle cinnamon sticks and secure with a strip of colorful ribbon. To each ribbon, attach a small ''harvest moon'' cut from white art board. Inscribe guests' names in gold ink.

ENTERTAINMENT:
Once again, music helps set the mood and add to the fun. If you do not have a piano in your home, make arrangements in advance to have music taped. Provide your pianist with a list of songs pertaining to the moon. Following dinner, your guests will enjoy a beautiful medley of music and delight in the challenge of naming each song. Remind them that each selection relates to the moon in some way. After they have finished guessing, provide lyrics for singing.

The following are possible musical choices: *Moon Over Miami, By the Light of the Silvery Moon, Shine On, Harvest Moon, It Must Have Been Moonglow, Moonlight and Roses.*

MENU:

Corn Chowder*
Assorted Lettuce Leaves With
Vinegarette Dressing
Cornish Hens*
Wild Rice
Apple Spice Cake*
Or
Pumpkin Roll*

To present the corn chowder in a very festive way, choose fairly small pumpkins, one for each guest. Carefully remove the stem area then hollow and clean each pumpkin inside and outside. Cover them loosely with a clean kitchen towel or plastic wrap and refrigerate to keep fresh. Bring the pumpkins to room temperature before serving, then fill the pumpkin cavities with corn chowder. For each guest, purchase a grapevine wreath the approximate size of your dinner plates. Carefully nestle each pumpkin/soup bowl inside a placesetting wreath. Tuck a cluster of chrysanthemums or a few autumn leaves into the wreaths for color.

MEMENTO:
Choose ornamental gourds, miniature pumpkins, squash, etc. as festive fall mementoes for your guests.

🍎 Back to School Bash 🍎

For a mother's celebration, a teacher appreciation luncheon or simply a great school send-off, this party theme can be adapted to almost any age group.

INVITATION:
Purchase small blackboards (approximately 10 inches in size) from a craft/discount store. Use white paint or real chalk protected with a spray sealant to "write" your invitation. Deliver to your guests in plain brown bags stenciled with apples and embellished with tufts of red tissue paper.

🍎 Back·To·School·Bash🍎

September 2, 1989   12 noon
at The Porters
14 Meadowlake

MOOD SET:
Use anything from the almost limitless source of school supplies: notebooks, pencils, paper, crayons, scissors, dictionaries, glue, textbooks, etc. to arrange an easy tablescape. Randomly place polished apples among the supplies. Core some of the apples and set votive or tea-light candles inside. Use other cored apples to hold miniature arrangements of flowers.

For an informal luncheon or supper, serve the meal in a variety of disposable containers (Chinese take-out buckets, small gift boxes or bags) placed inside brown lunch sacks. Repeat the apple stencil on the front of each bag and top the bags with fluffy red tissue paper. Secure a yellow pencil to each set of silverware, that has been wrapped in a red napkin and tied with brown twine. Table linens should continue the red and white motif.

ENTERTAINMENT:
If possible, have an ensemble from your local school choir, band or theater arts department share their talents.

For a gathering of teachers, have each one tell or write down an amusing story from his teaching experiences. Some of these stories will seem unbelievable - except to fellow teachers.

If this party is for a group of moms, have each one tell why she is ready for school to begin again.

For a children's party, play a relay game with chalkboard erasers or a round of bite-the-apple-on-the-string. Attach a length of string to a fresh red apple, and then secure the free end to the ceiling or other sturdy overhead structure. Prepare an apple for each child in this manner. With their hands behind their backs the children are to begin eating their apples when a signal is given. You may award a prize to the youngster consuming the most apple within the time limit.

MENU:
Keep in mind that this food selection must be suited to service in a sack.

A to Zucchini Bread Finger Sandwiches*
Teacher's Pet Pear Salad*
Toasted Pecans*
Applesauce Spice Cake*
Hot Spiced Tea or Iced Tea

MEMENTO:
Choose any apple-themed memento: an apple-scented candle, an apple magnet, spice bags for apple pie, or a tea towel with an apple applique.

Sunset Sonata Sangria

Illuminated by sunset, a strolling violinist sends strains of a sonata drifting through the early evening air. You and your guests will toast this intimate gathering and truly relax as romantic twilight soothes the soul.

INVITATION:

Select sheet music for a favorite sonata and duplicate onto parchment paper to give a rich, aged feel. On the reverse side of each invitation, in calligraphy if possible, inscribe party details.

Please join us
to enjoy
Sensuous Sunset
Soft Sonatas
&
Sweet Sangria
305 Waterside
~ Sunset ~
The Cains' Gazebo

MOOD SET:

Assemble the guests in an area inside or outside that captures the natural beauty of the sunset and sets the mood for intimacy and relaxation. Guests will enjoy mingling as the strolling violinist entertains with beautiful melodies. The furniture grouping and general arrangement of your entertainment area should be conducive to easy conversation. The simple theme of this party lends itself to a guest list of any size. If you plan on a large number of guests, consider using several buffet tables to better accommodate serving and to avoid congestion.

Use off-white table coverings and napkins. Take a look around the house, and gather objects that will hold center stage: antique lace runners or swags, old sheet music, strings of pearls, an antique violin, wide velvet or satin ribbon, a conductor's baton or off-white votive candles nestled in wine glasses will direct the mood toward charm and romance, and combine to make a lovely tablescape.

The sangria-filled punch bowl may be encircled with fruit or greenery and interspersed with small flowers and baby's breath. The buffet table is complete with the addition of china, wine glasses, and silver hors d'oeuvre trays filled with an elegant assortment of foods.

ENTERTAINMENT:

Contact your local high school, college or church music department or a professional musician's union for references to retain a violinist.

MENU:

Sangria*
Assorted Crackers and Cheese
Fruit Platter
Cheesy Apricot Dip*
Pineapple Cheese Ball*
Pumpernickel Bread Squares
Chicken Kabobs
Hot Mustard Sauce*

MEMENTO:

Bottle your own sangria for each couple. Decorate the bottle with ecru ribbons and attach a card or your own private label, suggesting that the couple enjoy a future sunset together. You may want to include the recipe for the sangria.

If your sunset view is truly a spectacular one, hire a professional photographer to photograph each couple against the breathtaking background. Mail the photos with a personal note later.

Raunchy Riverside Adventure

Here's a rip-roaring way to combine an outrageous party with the flavor of the 1800s. The mighty Mississippi River takes center stage for this party, even though you may be a thousand miles from its shore. Your home will become a crude riverbank saloon where a host of characters will gather. You might host gamblers, fur trappers, unsavory keelboatmen and flatboatmen, skalawags, swindlers and many floozie women.

INVITATION:
This poem, either duplicated or handwritten, will grab attention if you include a few playing cards or poker chips, a frilly garter or a red turkey feather, which historically symbolizes bravery and strength.

Mississippi River mud oozing
between your toes,
A riverside adventure is how this
party goes.
From days gone by when river life was tough
With gamblers, floozies, and boatmen so rough.
Come as a character, any baudy sort,
Shenanigans begin at 7 at The Smith's
River Port.
John & Wilma Smith 7087 Ridgeview Oct. 11

MOOD SET:

Your goal is to reflect the atmosphere of a rustic riverbank saloon. To create the essence of the Mississippi River, collect cattails and long river grasses from lake areas and fields and "plant" them in pots of plaster. Then, display cane poles, minnow or worm buckets, straw hats (Huckleberry Finn style), lanterns, whiskey bottles, banjos, garters, fur hides and gambling apparatus. Achieve a saloon interior with tattered oil-cloth tablecoverings, candles in rusted tin cans and unmatched silverware. Make your own napkins from inexpensive red gingham fabric.  Background music, either taped or live, will intensify the rowdiness if you choose frisky ragtime sounds. Beg, borrow, but don't steal enough cast-iron skillets to provide one for each guest. Serve a bounty of Southern treats in each skillet. Since much of the food will be cooked outside, the aroma of frying catfish and hushpuppies will add to the charm. Tin cups or mason jars can be used for beverages.

ENTERTAINMENT:

A contest to select the Flooziest Woman or the Cockiest Man will lend zest to the evening.

Game tables for poker, dice or any other gambling vices will get the group rumbling. Provide play money and any other equipment needed for your choice of games.

Or, if your guests are enthusiastic, have a "spitting" contest with watermelon seeds.

MENU:
With this irresistible meal, it will certainly be an evening not to count calories or cholesterol.

Hush-Your-Mouth Hushpuppies*
Purple Onion Rings
Crispy Fried Catfish Filets
Tomato Jack*
Watermelon Chunks
Mississippi Mud Pie*

MEMENTO:
For the ladies, fill small bags with the dry ingredients for hush-your-mouth hushpuppies. Secure each bag with twine and insert a red turkey feather. Present each gentleman with a new deck of cards.

Reflections

At this elegant but intimate dinner party, your dining table will be bathed in gleaming silver and "reflective mirrors." Your guests will be dazzled by the dramatic effect, as well as a delicious meal followed by moments of personal reflection.

INVITATION:
An exquisite invitation written in silver ink will be a distinctive prelude to this party. Enclose with each invitation a small, silver decoration, perhaps a stuffed heart or star made of silver lamé. Nestle each decoration and invitation in tufts of silver paper and place in a silver gift bag. Personally deliver the invitations/bags.

> ## Reflections...
> ## a Dinner Party!
>
> September 2, 1990   7:30 p.m.
>
> ### The Millers
> 123 Bayview

MOOD SET:
Sheets of mylar or a large mirror placed in the center of the table will provide a reflective base for your tablescape. Add candles (glittered if possible), beads (the type made for Christmas tree decorations) and swirls of ribbon, all in silver, of course. With silver spray paint you can transform eucalyptus, baby's breath, dried flowers and clusters of plastic fruits or flowers into lustrous additions for the tablescape. Even ordinary, inexpensive straw placemats will shimmer with a coat of silver paint.

If a chandelier is centered over the table, drape lengths of silver ribbon from the chandelier to each place setting. Then, anchor each strip with the guest's silver-wrapped memento. Tie silver bows on the side of each guest chair and attach a placecard to the center of each bow. Your best china, crystal and silver will triumph in this fairy tale setting.

If possible, hire a harpist, string quartet or pianist to provide sophisticated background music. Otherwise, taped classical music will substitute nicely.

ENTERTAINMENT:
Instead of merely writing guests' names on placecards, consider a more challenging way to seat your guests. Using a dictionary or encyclopedia, find a definition of each name or portion of a name. For example, for the name ''Shelley'' write, ''an explosive artillery projectile.'' This definition is taken from the word ''shell.'' Use your imagination to create entertaining placecards.

A second activity requires that each guest complete a questionnaire. You may choose to do this activity just before dessert is served. Share your answers.

1. Other than your children or marriage, name something of which you are proud.

2. How did you spend your last birthday?

3. What do you think is the biggest distortion about how others perceive you?

4. What book are you presently reading?

MENU:

Vegetable Cheese Soup*
Fresh Spinach Salad*
Mediterranean Chicken*
Sautéed Vegetables
Wheat Rolls
Chocolate Amaretto Cheesecake*
Hand-Dipped Chocolate Strawberries

MEMENTO:

As a remembrance of this stunning dinner party, give each guest a miniature silver picture frame wrapped in silver paper. Remember that this memento is to be incorporated into the tablescape as previously discussed.

Be True To Your School

Here's an amusing and enlightening way to learn more about your friends and their high school (or college) days. When each guest arrives dressed as the mascot of his school, the howls and giggles will begin.

INVITATION:
Use craft felt to shape school pennants and attach to dowel rods. With fabric paint, write your invitation on the pennants. Deliver in person or mail in mailing tubes.

Be True to Your School
On October 3 at 7:00 p.m.,
come dressed as your
high school mascot!
The Longs
214 Trail Ln.

45

MOOD SET:

Go immediately to your attic, basement or closet. Find that old letter jacket, megaphone, football, basketball or band instrument, as well as photos, clippings, yearbooks and scrapbooks. Use these items and more pennants to set your tablescape. Coordinate your table covering with your own school colors.

Display record album covers from your youth and a map with each guest's hometown marked with a tiny pennant. Play favorite old records for background music.

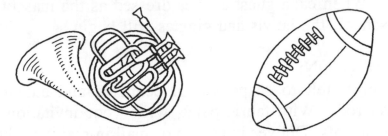

Plastic trays (approximately 9"×12") reminiscent of drive-ins, carhops or even school cafeterias will be amusing serving dishes. Serve bottled beverages from days gone by.

ENTERTAINMENT:

The evening will progress with a natural hoopla as each person sings, hums or whistles his own school song.

Involve your guests in an activity that requires completion of the following questionnaire. Collect the responses and read them one at a time. Have your guests guess whose answers are whose.

1. Name and describe your senior English teacher.
2. What was the funniest thing that happened to you as a high school student?
3. What kind of car did you drive in high school?
4. Where was your Senior Prom held and who was your date?
5. Who was the Homecoming Queen? What is she doing now?

Before the party, ask each guest to send a photo from his high school days. Duplicate these photos and compile your own program or yearbook. Add little-known facts about each guest. Have a time for autographing.

MENU:
Aside from reminiscing, the best part of this party is its simplicity. The menu should reflect both aspects.

Chili Dogs and Toppings

Tater Tots and Chips

Rah-Rah Relishes

Chocolate Chip Cookies to Cheer For*

Bottled Beverages

Milkshakes or Malts

Serve the chili dogs in paper liners and top each one with a pennant made of toothpick and paper.

MEMENTO:
The program/yearbook that you compile will be a great reminder of this light-hearted party.

When winter days grow long and dreary, brighten the mood with colorful quilts and a comfortable blend of good friends. Your guests will love snuggling up for a cozy evening by the fire.

INVITATION:
Use art board or purchase plain commercial notecards for your invitations. Trace a simple pattern (a heart, a star or rectangle) onto the front cover of each invitation. Using small, sharp craft scissors or a craft knife, carefully cut out the shape from the front covers of the invitations; do not penetrate through to the backs. Select a piece of quilted fabric. Glue a small swatch of the quilted fabric onto the inside of the covers so that the opening is filled with fabric. Inscribe the following message:

Winter eves grow cold & long;
A roaring fire brings pleasure.
Fine food & wine we'll gladly serve
Just bring a quilt you treasure.

Dinner served fireside
7:30 p.m.
January 19 th
The Mills 1304 Stonebridge

MOOD SET:

The warm cozy glow from the fireplace, and the flicker of numerous candles will be a welcome reprieve for guests on a chilly winter evening. Prior to your guests' arrival, rearrange or remove furniture to allow maximum room for spreading the quilts. Lounging before a magnificent, crackling fire with good wine and soothing music will set the tone for relaxed conversation. Invite guests to select a basket from your serving table and return to the fireside to discover and enjoy its contents.

Cover your dining table with one or more quilts and select napkins and tableware in complementary colors. Candles and a casual arrangement of fresh flowers are all you need to complete this tablescape, which focuses on the quilts. For unique candle holders, purchase inexpensive balls of yarn and thread. Carefully nestle a candle inside each.

Prepare a meal in a basket for each guest. Use an assortment of your favorite small baskets or purchase baskets especially for this party. Line the baskets with fabric that complements the color scheme established in the quilts. Fill the baskets with delicious but easy-to-handle meals. Add condiments and the necessary flatware, tableware and napkins.

ENTERTAINMENT:
While enjoying coffee and dessert, encourage guests to share the heritage of the quilt they brought.

Easy listening music or classical selections might be played softly throughout the evening.

MENU:

Carrot and Celery Bundles
Black Bean Soup*
Bread Loaves
Pumpkin Bread*

Do not include the dessert in the baskets; instead, serve later with coffee and brandy.

MEMENTO:

The baskets from which the meal was served will make nice mementoes.

You might choose from the wide variety of quilted items readily available at craft shows, antique shops, etc. Quilted pillows, animals, necklaces, pins or picture frames will carry out the quilt theme and be a wonderful treasure for each guest.

Cookie House Brunch

With so many adult parties happening at Christmas time, children often feel left out of the festivities. Here's an idea to include both children and adults--A Cookie House Brunch--where each family will create a spectacular no-bake Cookie House (a much simpler version of a gingerbread house).

INVITATION:
From plain brown grocery bags or brown craft paper make cookie house invitations. Fold each sheet so that the folded edge forms the roof as illustrated.

For each invitation, cut a house shape and decorate it with markers depicting cookies and candy such as vanilla wafers, gum drops, graham crackers and peppermints. Children will love to get involved with this activity. Open the house and write on the inside:

At Christmastime when life gets so busy
It's easy to feel lost and in a tizzy!
So we are hosting a Cookie House Brunch
A relaxing morning for your family bunch!
We hope you'll come..We'll have a surprise
That will add a twinkle to the children's eyes!

Date: Time:
Place:

53

MOOD SET:

Cover individual card tables with Christmas linens. The tables will serve first as dining tables and then as working surfaces for the cookie house projects. Disposable plates with a festive Christmas motif will make the clean-up easy. There are many on the holiday market from which to choose. For each place setting, tuck a sprig of evergreen under a pretty Christmas plaid ribbon and tie a bow around the silverware and napkin. Place an undecorated wooden house structure (as described in "Entertainment") in the center of each guest table. Label each house with a family's name. Have small baskets lined with red napkins or Christmas fabric to hold the cookies and candy you will use for decorating. Fill sundae dishes with peppermint sticks. Tie a ribbon onto the stem of each dish.

Poinsettias, candles, bows and the decorated Christmas tree will set the mood. Also, softly play Christmas music in the background for a merry touch.

ENTERTAINMENT:

The primary activity, other than socializing of course, is the creation of each family's cookie house. To facilitate the decorating process, it is wise to provide each family with a wooden house structure that you have previously built. Balsa wood or plywood can be easily cut to form a house shell approximately 10 inches wide and 12 inches high. With a glue gun you can attach the front, back, sides and roof. There is no need to cut windows or doors since these will later be made with cookies and candy. This shell will make a stable base for a cookie house.

Supply a variety of packaged cookies (vanilla wafers, graham crackers, etc.) and icing (either store-bought or homemade). All family members can contribute their talents to create a special cookie house. Use the icing like glue to secure shingles, bricks, windows and doors made of cookies and candy. Be certain that no wood is left exposed.

MENU:
Since this is a brunch for children as well as adults, the food selections are geared to please both.

Warm Winter Fruit Salad*
Spicy Blueberry Muffins
Quicky Quiche*
Assorted Donuts and Pastries
Merry Berry Juice*
Mimosas For Adults

MEMENTO:
Each family will treasure their cookie house as a memento.

Wine Down

This is a post-Christmas holiday party perfect for sagging spirits, weary women, moping mommies, or any combination of friends who might need to just "wine down."

INVITATION:
Make your own invitations as shown. Use art board for the bottle shape. Affix a label and inscribe the invitation. Decorate with holly berries to add holiday spirit. Or purchase commercial invitations with a holiday design or note cards with a wine or grape motif.

A time to relax and chase the blues, December 29th is the date we choose. From a busy Christmas you must rebound, Stop by at 4 – we'll just... Wine Down

MOOD SET:

A warm and welcoming fire, good friends, smooth wine, soothing musical selections and holiday greenery, poinsettias, etc. provide a pleasing atmosphere. Your tablescape might consist of a collection of wine bottles plus any unique bottles or jars. Slip single blossoms or branches into some of the bottles and adorn others with ribbons and bits of lace. Be ingenious with your choices; take a peek around your own landscape or nearby wooded acreage for berries, evergreens, etc.

ENTERTAINMENT:

It is not necessary to plan elaborate entertainment; the relaxing atmosphere will be conducive to easy conversation among friends.

MENU:
Assorted Crackers and Cheese
Toasted Pecans*
Fruit Tray
Pineapple Cheese Ball*
Wine
Soft Drinks

MEMENTO:

Purchase tiny bottles available in most import stores or party supply stores. Or, purchase corks, decorate and affix a magnet to each for a handy memento.

Gilded Gala

The brilliance of gleaming gold and shimmering silver will cast a lustrous glow on this dinner party. Celebrate old friendships and cultivate new ones during an elegant evening touched by King Midas himself.

INVITATION:

Order a formal printed invitation or write your own, on elegant white paper using gold ink. Mail in customary form, or personally deliver to each guest, presenting the invitation on a silver tray. Formal attire lends an unexpected touch of elegance to the personal delivery. When compiling your guest list, remember that each couple receiving an invitation will in turn invite a couple.

Make new friends but keep the old
One is Silver ~ the other is Gold.
The bond of our friendship so dear we hold
The joys, the treasures, old friends ~ The Gold.
Bring a new pair ~ The Silver we need
New friendships like flowers must begin
with a seed.

Date ~ Time ~ Place ~

Please invite a couple with whom you have recently become acquainted. R.S.V.P.

MOOD SET:

Your "Gilded Gala" can be achieved effectively without breaking the bank. Utilize the many marvelous treasures so often confined to display cabinets or storage: finest flatware, china, linens, serving pieces and expresso cups. The tablescape begins when you drape your dining table with gold lamé or lace. You may want to cover chairbacks with a similar swathe. A host of flickering candles casts an iridescent glow over everything. Use a medley of white candles in an elegant array of unusual holders: silver wine goblets or silver baby cups, small golden bowls, vases, tea-cups and other imaginative serving pieces. You will certainly want to incorporate your fine silver candlesticks or candelabrum with the tablescape. A silver champagne bucket brimming with white narcissus will lend a luscious, romantic aroma.

Utilize any gold or silver serving pieces, gold and silver doilies, etc., when presenting the meal. Gold beads, coins, a sterling baby rattle, or grandmother's handmirror, a pillbox, an atomizer or any other unique pieces rich in gilt will complete the mood.

60

ENTERTAINMENT:
A careful blend of old and new friends in your seating assignments will help ensure interesting conversation. Hire a professional pianist, harpist or three-piece ensemble to provide wonderful dinner music. You may want to conclude this regal evening with dancing.

MENU:

Avocado - Shrimp Salad*
Sesame Chicken with Red Plum Sauce*
Seasoned Rice
Steamed Asparagus Spears
Herbed Dinner Rolls*
Gilded Almond Delights*

MEMENTO:
A glittering token of friendship as extravagant or as economical as your budget allows is sure to please. The memento you choose may become part of the tablescape, placed at each guest's place setting. Or, you may present the gift to each guest from a gilded basket or box upon departure. Make gold lamé jewel pouches or transform small inexpensive boxes into treasure chests by applying fabric or paint.

Dinner with the Captain

Your guests will board the S.S. Buchanan (fill in your last name) via a ship's ramp. Once on deck, the steam whistle will blast, and you will depart for your favorite port-of-call. Even more intriguing about this tongue-in-cheek episode is that your guests will double as members of the Captain's crew. Bon Voyage!

INVITATION:

This fabulous sailing requires formal custom-printed invitations like those used on real cruise liners. Check your local printer for a selection of high-quality stationery. An ivory card bordered in blue or red with coordinating ink would be most appropriate.

Captain Joseph Smith
cordially invites you for

Cocktails & Dinner
at his table

Departing Saturday, May 29, 1991
7:00 P.M.
aboard the
S.S. Buchanan   *R.S.V.P.*

<u>MOOD SET</u>:
This party requires some worthwhile effort but certainly is not complicated. With a bounty of inspiration, your home will become the interior of a luxury cruise ship from bow to stern. Leading your guests to the front door, a ramp constructed of budget-priced lumber will introduce this cruise fantasy.

A string of nautical flags stretched alongside the ramp will add to the intrigue. Once inside, the Captain (the party host) and the Cruise Director (the party hostess) will greet each passenger.

The Captain, regally dressed in uniform, and the Cruise Director, dressed in formal attire, will give each passenger a cocktail, a package of spiraling paper streamers and a surprise card. (Explanation of these ''surprise cards'' will follow in Entertainment.) For a special touch, serve cocktails on napkins printed with your ship's name.

A stately-dressed dining room will become the perfect setting for this extraordinary experience. Set your table in grandeur with fine china, crystal, silver and crisp, white linens. Any of these can be easily rented, and they promise to create an elegant mood. An arrangement of fresh-cut flowers is an appropriate centerpiece.

After cocktails have been served, the steam whistle will blast (pre-record your own variation). Everyone will throw their streamers and toast a memorable cruise. Now the *real* party will begin.

ENTERTAINMENT:

As previously mentioned, every guest will be given a "surprise card." Each card will give a description of a member of the cruise staff. The evening's drama will unfold and the fun will begin as each guest assumes his role. Here are some character suggestions:

The Purser - You are to check with each guest to see if any "valuables" (purses, money, coats, jewelry, etc.) are in need of being "locked up." Use your imagination.

The Photographer - You are to photograph each couple with the Captain. Ask the Cruise Director for the camera and further directions.

Maitre d' - You are to seat each couple at the Captain's table according to the placecards. Begin this procedure when the dinner chimes softly ring.

Chief Fire Officer - You will inspect each guest immediately following the Fire Alarm. Check to see that life jackets are being worn correctly. This ought to be fun.

Flambé Chef - You will ignite and serve the meal's grand finale, a flaming dessert, at the instruction of the Captain.

Wine Steward - After the Captain presents you with a ribboned-medallion, you will pour the wine for each course of the meal. Check with the Cruise Director for further instruction.

Table Steward - You will graciously serve the meal, remove the plates and use the crumb brush between courses. Also, it is your special assignment to unfold and place napkins in the guests' laps as they are seated.

Dance Instructor - At the conclusion of the meal, all guests will enter the Grand Ballroom for instruction. Choose the Mambo, the Cha-cha, the Waltz or any other dance steps for demonstration and instruction. The Cruise Director will provide appropriate taped music.

If you have more guests, consider some of these characters as well: 1st Mate, bus boy, cabaret comedian, magician, hypnotist or showgirl.

Excitement and laughter will fill your ship as your guests tackle their role play assignments throughout the evening.

Sound effects for a cruise ship can be achieved through a bit of imagination. The low-pitched steam whistle might be reproduced by a hefty blow on a bottle. A xylophone played with a soft mallet can become the gentle dinner chimes. The sound of the fire alarm might be made by a clanging alarm clock.

66

As previously mentioned, a gold medallion with ribbon will be needed to place around the neck of the Wine Steward. For your staff you will need an instant camera, a crumb brush and dance selections. You will also need a life jacket for every guest.

The order of the evening will be maintained by the Captain and the Cruise Director. During cocktails, the ship's photographer will take a photo of each couple with the Captain. Remember, at the blast of the steam whistle everyone will throw streamers, and the Captain will propose a toast. Then he should explain the ship's creative "Fire Drill" procedure. Have the life jackets nearby. As the fire alarm clangs, everyone will scurry around trying to secure life jackets. The sight of finely dressed men and women adorned with bulky life jackets will set a jolly tone for the evening. After life jackets have been cinched, The Chief Fire Officer will begin his "inspections."

Immediately following the "inspection" will be the chimes announcing dinner. The Maitre d' should state, "Dinner is now being served in the Captain's Dining Room." Excitement will fill the air as the Maitre d' seats each couple.

After everyone is seated, the Captain should summon the Wine Steward for the ceremony in which the medallion is placed around the Steward's neck. The Wine Steward will then pour the selected wine while The Table Steward serves the appetizer.

Obviously, it is mandatory that the food for this party be prepared in advance. The Cruise Director will oversee the Wine Steward and Table Steward and the progress of the various dinner courses. Most probably the guests playing the roles of the Wine Steward and Table Steward will be chided and good-naturedly teased as they busy themselves with their duties. When it is time for the flaming dessert to be served, the Flambé Chef will assume his role.

At the conclusion of this memorable meal, the Captain and Cruise Director will lead the guests to a room large enough for dancing. The Dance Instructor and his partner will be called upon to give their demonstration and instruction. Then all guests are invited to join in the fun until your ship arrives at its destination.

MENU:

Chilled Fresh Shrimp Cocktail
Corn Chowder*
Green Salad
Alaskan King Salmon*
with Raspberry-Honey Sauce*
Gingered Carrots, Zucchini, and
Parsleyed New Potatoes
Raspberry Mousse*

MEMENTO:
A printed copy of the menu or the itinerary is appropriate.

Southwestern Fiesta

The spicy flavor of this Southwestern party is HOT! Pastel cacti, chili peppers and frozen margaritas set the pace for this memorable evening.

INVITATION:

For festive invitations, print a note on simple, brown paper and use raffia (available at any craft store) to attach the invitations to the stems of inexpensive margarita glasses. Use pinking shears to cut the edges of the tags.

A Southwestern Fiesta with a spicy flair,
Laughter and music will fill the air.
March 5th is the chosen day,
After siesta, we will dine ... Ole !

Casa de Langer
8:00 p.m.

Place the invitation/glass in a pastel gift bag and cushion it with tufts of coordinating tissue paper. Personally deliver each bag.

MOOD SET:
Decorative items of southwestern design are not difficult to locate. Check first with family and friends for Southwestern rugs, weavings, pottery, baskets and jewelry to enhance the festive mood. Fabrics in a contemporary Southwestern motif are readily available at most fabric stores and can be used as tablecoverings or basket liners, or may even be draped over furniture.

Put a pastel twist to the color scheme with tables set in shades of pink, purple and blue hues. Bandanas in these colors can be purchased for use as napkins. Small clusters of artificial peppers, spray painted in theme colors and tied with raffia or ribbon, will make great napkin ornaments. Attach other bandanas and peppers to a twig wreath for the front door to make a Southwestern welcome.

Inexpensive straw placemats can be spray painted in theme colors as well. Invert terra-cotta flower pots and saucers with or without glass hurricane lamps for festive candleholders. Intertwine raffia and accent with additional pepper clusters for a spicy tablescape!

For Southwestern charm, make several free-standing cacti out of wood, or check your local art stores and craft shows where unfinished cut-outs are available. Use your imagination to vary the sizes and shapes. Then, paint each cactus to coordinate with your pastel theme. No need for ordinary green cacti at this Fiesta - even polka-dotted or striped cacti are appropriate! Group some on tables or at the front door. Be sure to line your driveway and walkway with luminaries. To make luminaries fill lunch sacks with 2 inches of sand. Set a votive candle inside each. Background music with a Southwestern tempo will complete the mood.

ENTERTAINMENT:
Some like it hot! So, if you are very daring, try a jalepeno-eating contest...but have lots of water and saltine crackers available.

MENU:
Quick Quesadilla Appetizers
Spicy Black Beans
Layered Chicken Enchilada Casserole*
Best Ever Pralines*
Frozen Margaritas

MEMENTO:
Choose any Southwestern-theme gift: a jar of special hot sauce, blue corn chips or a batch of special pralines to take home.

A Family Affair

Perhaps no gathering is quite as memorable as the reunion of family. With some advance planning, you can host a Family Affair that will keep Aunt Bea gabbing for years.

INVITATION:
A pen and ink drawing of the old family homestead or a special heirloom will make a meaningful invitation to each guest. Or, make copies of an old family photo. Add a poem for unique bargain invitations.

Our Jordan clan is quite a bunch!
    Let's celebrate with fun and lunch.
We'll share thoughts of days gone by
With Aunt Lou's bread & Grandma's pie.
Please bring your favorite foods to share.
We'll spread a feast ~ a dieter's dare.
On May 12th at straight
        up 10,
That's when the games
    and frolic begin!
Hosted by:
Address:

Be certain to provide a map for out-of-town relatives.

MOOD SET:
The location and atmosphere of this party will be dictated by the number of extended family members and by the season. A back lawn, church or community hall may be an appropriate site. Also, many state and local parks have pavilions that can be reserved for such occasions. Most importantly, remember that you will need plenty of space for both adults and children and that you may need an alternate plan in case of bad weather.

A family banner, either homemade or commercially-produced, makes a warm greeting as family members arrive.

Nametags written in large, easy-to-read print are a great asset. It may also be beneficial to give a "relation explanation," especially if some relatives will be more unfamiliar than others. For example: Jane Jordan--James and Sally's daughter.

You can even make your own nametags from poster board or self-sticking shelf paper.

As relatives arrive with scrumptious goodies in hand, have extra coolers to store those dishes that need to be chilled. Having access to a microwave and conventional oven is helpful, too. Be certain to provide adequate buffet and guest tables. Cover tables in coordinating fabrics or sheets. Display groupings of family photos intertwined with curling ribbon or greenery for an easy but sentimental tablescape. Quilts spread on the ground can provide picnic-style seating for the children.

Silverware wrapped in coordinating napkins and tied with more curling ribbon may facilitate carrying plates and cups to the table.

Decorate a "family tree" by cutting out red apples from poster board. Label each apple with a member's name. Tie these apples on a nearby tree.

ENTERTAINMENT:
The following activities require some advance planning, but they are well worth the effort.

A Family Cookbook--A collection of favorite recipes is quite a treasure. Several months prior to the reunion, ask each family member to send recipes (accompanied by any special remembrances.) Organize the recipes and duplicate. Also, use drawings created by the young folks to illustrate food categories. Based on your cost limits, choose a cover type: notebook-style binder, plastic spiral, laminated poster board, etc. Family members will cherish this special book for years to come.

A Family Remembrance--Similar to the cookbook, this is a collection of memories. In advance, ask each family member to send written remembrances of family gatherings. It is especially fun to have members of the older generations explain how certain family traditions began or what life was like when they were youngsters. Include thoughts from the young family members, too. Duplicate and illustrate this book as is described for the Family Cookbook. You will have a legacy of love.

A Family Video--Gather significant old home movies, slides, or snapshots from relatives. Engage the services of a professional to transfer these to video cassette tapes, and make a copy for each family. A family history on video will make an invaluable memento.

A Family T-Shirt--Secure T-shirt sizes for each family member. By purchasing a large quantity of shirts, you should be able to save money. Then choose a design, phrase or logo to be printed on each shirt. The children would love to help with this. The result will be a wearable treasure.

Family Trivia Test--Make and duplicate a fun trivia test about family members. The difficulty of questions should be based on how well the members already know each other. Give everyone a test page and pencil.

Sample Questions:
1. What family member has the middle name "Gertrude"?
2. What family member was the first to graduate from college?
3. What couple married on Christmas Day?
4. What family member visited Alaska last summer?
5. What family member played a tuba in high school?

Now, here are some ideas specifically for the youngsters. These do not require advance planning.

1. Have the children write their own "family rap." They will love to tease and poke fun at their elders.
2. Have the children produce and film their own video of the day's activities. They could include songs, interviews and cheers.

3. Have the children organize tournaments of softball, croquet, soccer, horseshoes, badminton, volleyball etc.
4. Have the older children help the younger ones fly kites.

Last, but certainly not least, be sure to have several family members act as official photographers to capture the magic moments of this special day.

Singing Waiter Dinner

Your guests will adore the aura of a cozy Italian cafe. A tuxedoed waiter (either a friend or a professional) sings while he serves the evening's delights.

INVITATION:

Here's a unique musical invitation that will fascinate your guests. To the tune of *O Solo Mio,* record or videotape a singing invitation for each guest. The words of the invitation will substitute for the lyrics. If you choose not to create a singing invitation, copy the poem and a drawing of the waiter. Duplicate, tri-fold, address and mail to your guests.

We'll host a party
We hope you'll come
A singing waiter . . .
And lots of fun!
Lasagna at straight up 8
On April 12th, let's make a date.
The Andersons

MOOD SET:

Of course, the most essential element of this party is the waiter. If you have a talented friend with a sense of humor who is willing to share his singing ability, then by all means ask him. If you are not so fortunate, retain a professional. Obviously, you will also need a piano and accompanist.

Once you have secured your musicians, this evening of merriment will be well on its way to success. A week or two before the party, ask each guest to submit the name of his favorite tune. For a personal touch, supply your waiter and the accompanist this information so that they will be able to perform these special requests during the evening. You might even want to use these song titles as a novel way to address placecards. Instead of writing each guest's name on a placecard, write his favorite song title.

Then when it is time to be seated, have the guests pair together (no spouses together, though) and escort one another to their seats by guessing which song title belongs to whom.

A rich red, forest green and white color scheme for linens is effective. Use tables-for-four to create an intimate atmosphere. At each place setting lay a brass musical note. (You can often find these as Christmas ornaments.) Fill cored eggplants with arrangements of fresh flowers for centerpieces. Wine bottles covered with candle drippings and topped with tapers will be reminis-

cent of an old coffee house. Dimmed lights, background piano music and scrumptious lasagna dinner will strike a perfect chord.

After each course is served, the waiter can sing yet another request. It's an almost sure bet that before long your guests will be singing along.

ENTERTAINMENT:
Since this evening's festivity centers around the music and meal, no other activities are required.

MENU:

Sultry Garden Salad
Lusty Lasagna*
Italian Loaves
Marinated Strawberries in Rum*
Choice Wine
Gourmet Coffee

MEMENTO:
The brass musical note from the place setting will make a wonderful memento.

Give your boots a shine, and ride into the spirit of the wild west at this gathering of cowpokes. Good grub and toe tappin' tunes will have your guests hollerin' ''yee hah''!

INVITATION:
To lasso guests, cut a rope into one-foot lengths; tie a knot at both ends. Attach bright red invitations, purchased or cut from art board, inscribed with the following poem:

> It's a western round-up so starch your jeans.
> Mosey on over for some cowboy beans.
> The grub will be served 'round the Harper's campfire;
> There might be some dancin' before we retire.
> Cook says we'll eat 'round about eight.
> Lasso your partner and don't be late!
> 2406 Westway
> The Harpers

Coil the rope invitations and wrap in sheets of red and blue tissue paper. Place in large manila envelopes for mailing.

MOOD SET:

Use dark blue oil cloth or a light weight denim-look fabric to cover buffet and guest tables; pie tins and mason jars are novel tableware for this campfire-style meal. Tie silverware for each guest with red bandanas. The bandanas will serve as napkins. Shiny brass spittoons or cowboy boots will hold arrangements of daisies or wild flowers. Gather rope, lanterns, an old tin coffee pot and tin coffee cups and a few more red bandanas. Place two inches of sand in the bottom of a mason jar, then place a candle inside. Group several of these items for an attractive, inexpensive tablescape with western impact.

Guests will appreciate a proper wild west welcome. Raid the woodpile for branches or lumber to fashion a rustic hitching post. Position hay bales, saddles, bridles, rope, cowboy hats etc. at the entry to your home. Make a western wreath by attaching a cowboy boot to a grapevine wreath. For color tuck bandanas into the boot. Hang the simple yet effective cowboy wreath on the front door or other prominent location.

ENTERTAINMENT:

A professional country western band will liven up the evening and provide great music for dancing. Of course, there is an abundance of country western music available on tape.

If you have never done any country western dancing, hire an instructor for the evening; learning in a group can be great fun!

Provide song sheets so that your guests can join in a sing-along around the "campfire". Perhaps one of your guests plays guitar and would enjoy leading the fun. *Home on the Range, Deep in the Heart of Texas* and *Tumblin' Tumbleweed* are examples.

MENU:

Pinto Beans
Campfire Skillet Dinner*
Sliced Purple Onion Rings
Dill Pickle Spears
Fried Apricot Pies

MEMENTO:

Bolo ties for the men and a small piece of western inspired silver jewelry for the women will make welcome gifts. Nestle whatever gift you choose inside bandanas or denim fabric cut into squares. Bring the ends up together. Tie each gift pouch with twine.

Safari Soiree

You'll have fun if you monkey around with this party theme. Watch as your home is transformed into the wild lands of Africa. Your guests will arrive in exotic safari clothes or in costumes as savage beasts.

INVITATION:
Choose from several ideas:

On a Safari we will go
   to the jungles & plains, high & low
Come as an animal from the wild
   or as a hunter, man, woman, or child
On May 3 at 7:00 sharp
   From our camp
The expedition will start!

1. Glue imitation animal fabric onto blank notecards, cover them entirely and trim the fabric edges to match the cards. Write your invitation inside.

2. Glue paper circles over the lenses of toy binoculars. Write your invitation on the paper circles. Then place the binoculars in camouflaged gift bags and deliver in person.

3. Purchase inexpensive safari hats at a toy store or discount store. Place your handwritten invitation inside and deliver in person.

MOOD SET:

Achieve a safari atmosphere by draping yards of green netting from the ceiling. Twist folded lengths of green crepe paper into "vines." Make palm fronds by molding green pipe cleaners into leaf shapes and then gluing the pipe cleaners onto green crepe paper. Next, make the "fringe" by cutting slits into the leaf edges. Create "trees" by nailing dowel rods to small blocks of wood. Cover the dowels with tubes of brown corrugated cardboard or similar material. Attach several palm fronds to complete your trees. Also, use clusters of green balloons to make other tree tops.

Search your closets for appropriate stuffed animals: lions, tigers, zebras, elephants, giraffes, monkeys, etc. Drag out a green tent, tarpaulin, mosquito netting, lanterns, binoculars, safari hats or other equipment which would enhance your theme.

Cut imitation animal skin fabric into realistic skin shapes. Drape these over sofas or chairs. Use the same skin fabric to cover your dining table. Arrange the lanterns, safari hats, binoculars and a few stuffed animals for your tablescape. You may want to purchase camouflage disposable plates, cups and napkins for easy clean-up. Or choose solid white plates, decorating each with a palm frond.

ENTERTAINMENT:
Every safari traveler will enjoy a photo memento. Use your lush background as a focal point. Also consider making your own mini-frames from poster board and self-adhesive paper to create a wild jungle effect.

For an active participation activity, divide your guests into two teams and arrange them in two long lines. Designate the first person in each line as the "runner." Standing midway between the two teams, call out an object that each team member should look for on himself. Once any team member has the designated item, he must pass it down the line to the team runner. The runner must take it as quickly as possible to the host or hostess. The runner who arrives first with the item in hand wins a point for his team. Scavenger items to include: a false eye lash, a diamond ring, a college ring, a pair of glasses, a brown belt, a man's handkerchief, a social security card.

MENU:

Fruited Spears
Safari Stew*
Cornbread Muffins
Caramel Nut Brownies*

MEMENTO:

The photos of your safari guests will be a perfect reminder of this exciting evening.

two by two

Here's an amusing twist to an ordinary costume party.
Each couple will come dressed as a pair of animals
journeying to Noah's Ark. As Mr. or Mrs. Noah, you
will greet each pair of guests as they come on board just
before the flood begins. Two by two, they will come:
monkeys, giraffes, ducks or any critters that roamed the
earth.

INVITATION:

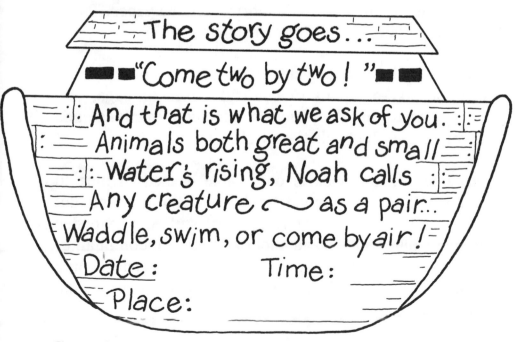

The story goes...
"Come two by two!"
And that is what we ask of you.
Animals both great and small
Water's rising, Noah calls
Any creature ～ as a pair...
Waddle, swim, or come by air!
Date: Time:
Place:

Copy the poem onto appropriate cards.

MOOD SET:
Construct a wooden ramp leading to your ark. Whether your ramp is inside or outside, the animals will know they have entered the ark when an appropriately attired Mr. and Mrs. Noah greet them.

To achieve the sense of a flood, play an environmental tape of a thunderstorm. Dim the lights as the flood waters rise, and use various candles and oil lamps for lighting. Then, set sail with a boatload of wild party animals.

Since the evening's format focuses on pairs, dinner should reflect the same theme. Dinner-for-two served in galvanized buckets is sure to suit every creature. Line the buckets with rainbow-bright fabric or tissue paper. Then, add coordinating bows to the handles.

The food will be packaged in whimsical containers: small Chinese take-out pails or colorful boxes or bags, and then placed in the buckets. Include napkins and silverware in the buckets as well.

Place the dinner buckets on a table draped in blue to resemble the water around Noah's ark. For a simple but effective tablescape, feature pairs of stuffed or wooden animals, blue candles and a lot of curling ribbon in all of the hues of the rainbow. Then, for a very casual dining experience, have your guests scatter onto quilts placed on the floor.

ENTERTAINMENT:

Your guests will delight in viewing each couple's costumes. Every animal pair should adore having a picture made with Mr. and Mrs. Noah. Establish a background and snap. Or, have your guests list things that usually come in "pairs" (i.e. twinkies, feet, double-dip-ice cream).

MENU:

Side-By-Side Sandwiches
Rainy Day Veggies and Dip
Floodwater Wafers*
Caramel Nut Brownies*

MEMENTO:

A "Tea for Two" gift basket should make an amusing memento. Use two inexpensive tea cups or mugs and tuck special tea bags inside.

A Young Lady's Birthday Tea Party

When a little girl receives this invitation for a tea time birthday celebration, she will feel like Cinderella! Dressed in her finest clothes, she will adore using her manners at this elegant party.

INVITATION:
Intricate paper dolls can become a marvelous invitation. Use a roll of white craft paper to create a succession of at least ten dolls for each invitation. Hand letter the poem on the last paper doll and place in an appropriate envelope. Use a gold seal or lace doily to seal the envelope for a special touch.

A birthday is a special day
For friends to come in a fancy way.
We'll have some tea & other treats
Frills and lace, snacks so sweet
We'll give a toast, we hope you'll come
For this birthday tea and grown-up fun!

Honoring:

Date:

Time:

Place:

MOOD SET:

Young ladies will feel oh-so grown-up when they use fine china and silver service at the formal dining table. Choose a pastel hue to repeat through the tablescape with ribbons, lace, flowers and linens. Because only tea and finger desserts will be served, each place setting should be limited to a tea cup, saucer and dessert plate. A large lace doily, either round or rectangular, can become a placemat. Use more crisp doilies for both the saucer and dessert plates.

A nosegay fashioned from tiny rosebuds and baby's breath will make each young lady feel grand! Form small bouquets of flowers and surround them with delicate, white tulle. Secure the bouquets with florist's wire and tape, and then add ribbon bows and streamers. Place a nosegay at each place setting. Provide placecards as well.

Favorite dolls or teddy bears can make special appearances when outfitted in their best clothes, hats and bows. Gather these together in a corner or position them individually in empty chairs. Some of the bears can even hold bouquets of pastel or white balloons.

96

ENTERTAINMENT:

To maintain an elegant atmosphere, provide only activities that require limited physical involvement. Certainly the young ladies will enjoy pictures of themselves with the birthday honoree. And, of course, the opening of birthday gifts remains a cherished tradition.

MENU:

Instead of serving birthday cake, try a selection of tea cakes, candy and gourmet cookies served from a silver tray. Purchased or homemade, they will thrill the young ladies.

Tea Party Tea Cakes*
Momentous Bon Bons*
Fruit Punch

MEMENTO:

The nosegay for each guest will make a delightful memento of this elegant afternoon.

Purple Passion Party

Let your child's interests, activities, hobbies or hang-ups spark your imagination in planning a party that you, your child and guests will long remember! For instance, a passion for purple can be played up and presented successfully if it is currently an important and fun part of your child's life.

INVITATION:
With purple ribbon or yarn, attach purple crayons or markers to white cards inscribed in purple as follows:

Purple Passion Party
A purple party is being planned,
We hope that you will be on hand.
Purple fun and purple food,
We hope you're in a purple mood!
A birthday full of "purpleness,"
Please do come in purple dress.
Date: Place:
Time:

MOOD SET:

An abundance of purple party paraphernalia is available: balloons, streamers, confetti, tissue paper, banners, paper and plastic goods, etc. Purple violets, pansies and a variety of silk flowers are perfect for planters, baskets or the tablescape. Use your imagination, and remember, if you are unable to locate a specific item in just the right color, you can paint, stencil, cover, tint or splatter. The possibilities are endless!

ENTERTAINMENT:

The following examples are appropriate for children approximately six to ten years of age.

Pass The Purple Cup Foot Relay--Divide the children into two teams of equal number. Make a row of chairs for each team. Children are seated, and a purple paper cup is placed between the toes of the first child on each team. At the signal the cup is passed to the next team member using only toes or feet. No hands allowed! The cup must be passed down the row and back. A purple prize may be awarded to winning team members.

100

Purple Partner Stunt--Each pair of children is given an inflated purple balloon. Facing one another, each pair is to carefully position the balloon between them. At the signal, each pair is to turn around so that the balloon remains between them back to back. No hands allowed! The children will quickly become very adept.

Older children might enjoy Purple Pictionary. Let them take turns drawing purple items on a large tablet while teammates guess what they are drawing. In advance, write on strips of paper the names of objects that could be purple and place the papers in a box. Artists will select a strip of paper then draw that object. Examples: grapes, grape juice, grape jelly, jellybeans, violets, Easter eggs, purple eye shadow, etc.

Keep your child's interests, activities or hobbies in mind when choosing other appropriate activities.

MENU:
This menu is for a sleep-over party.

Peanut Butter and Grape Jelly Finger Sandwiches
Chips
Birthday Cake or Cup Cakes
(decorated with purple icing, jellybeans, or tinted coconut)
Purple Cows*
(a simple recipe children will enjoy making themselves)

Purple Seedless Grapes
Blueberry Muffins
Toast
·Grape Jelly
Grape Juice

MEMENTO:
Fill purple party bags with purple pens, pencils, notebooks, diaries, address books, small stuffed animals, jellybeans, bath crystals, jewelry, etc. A handcrafted memento is always special. Let the children decorate their own purple passion t-shirts. Young ladies might especially enjoy painting or stenciling purple flowers, hearts, etc. on small white wicker baskets.

Keep This Under Your Hat

Everyone loves a secret. Careful planning and clever friends are crucial to the success of this individualized surprise party as you watch your guest of honor's life unfold through stories, photographs and music. Sssssh.....keep this under your hat.

INVITATION:

Select a hat style suitable for the mood you want to create: a formal black top hat, cowboy hat, baseball cap, tennis visor or old-time straw boater. Most are available at party or carnival supply stores, discount stores or sporting goods stores. Decorate the hats or caps of your choice with ribbon, flowers, feathers, etc. to establish your color scheme. Trace a pattern to fit the crown of each hat, then cut them out of white art paper to make your invitations.

Use ink matching your color scheme to write party details. Using a hot glue gun, secure the invitation to the inside crown of the hat or cap. Hand deliver your creations.

MOOD SET:
To greet your guests, hang one or more of the theme hats on the front door. In addition, baskets or clay pots filled with flowering plants or brightly colored balloons offer a festive greeting.

You might consider placing "hatsfull" of crackers, chips, nuts, popcorn, etc. in accessible locations throughout your entertaining area. Group theme hats, candles, lengths of ribbon, flowers, etc. to create an attractive tablescape. Select napkins, table covers, and dinnerware that complement the color scheme. Adorn guest tables with a matching hat and helium-filled balloons, or use a candle covered with a clear hurricane globe that is tied with more ribbon and flowers.

If you dine outdoors, use citronella candles in hurricane lawn lamps to help prevent pesky insects.

ENTERTAINMENT:
Advance preparation allows you the pleasure of enjoying this party with your guests and surprising a special friend with exciting entertainment. You will find this worth the time and effort it requires.

Include instructions with the invitations for each guest to provide *in advance* a baby picture of himself. Carefully number the pictures, and display them in a prominent location at the party. Provide paper and pens for the guests, and allow time for identifying the baby photos. This simple activity stimulates great fun and conversation during cocktails.

The first to correctly identify all photographs might receive a picture frame or another gift of your choice.

Following a buffet dinner, continue the birthday celebration with a "This is Your Life" type musical review. Secure photographs from relatives and friends exemplifying the life of your guest of honor. Have these photos made into slides. (Exercise great caution in seeing that photos and memorabilia are returned undamaged.) Ask for insights and recollections, verify dates and places and gather memorabilia, etc. that will assist you in composing an original "This is Your Life" script. With help from a talented friend or professional musician, set the slides and script to music. *Sentimental Journey, Magic Moments, Daddy's Little Girl, Baby Face, School Days,* favorite pop tunes, a college fight song and the *Wedding March,* are only a few of many possible selections; the key is to personalize. Use a little friendly persuasion to enlist some of your guests to take part in the musical production. The secret advance rehearsals will be as much fun as the party. Choose a few of the honoree's well-known hobbies, personality traits, habits, accomplishments, etc. that can be expressed in song.

You may compose original works or re-write the lyrics of familiar tunes that the special "guest stars" will perform to complement the slide presentation.

Your effort will make for a smashing success. This is a surprise party your friends won't "keep under their hats"....they will be talking about it for days.

MENU:
                    Sliced Baked Ham
                    Hot Mustard Sauce*
                    Sliced Beef Brisket
        Small Rolls Split in Half for Sandwiches
                    Artichoke Spread*
                    Pumpernickel Rounds
         Assorted Fresh Fruits and Vegetables
                    Apricot Squares*
                 Blueberry Cheesecake*

If your party is outdoors, you may want to ice canned drinks in an antique bathtub or other large novel container for a unique and convenient beverage service area.

MEMENTO:
Choose a colorful backdrop for taking an instant snapshot of each couple upon their arrival. Fill a special album for the guest of honor using these photographs and a personal birthday message inscribed by each guest.

Flamin' Forties Frolic

If you have exhausted all the "over the hill" black and white 40th birthday ideas, try this RED HOT revelry for a change.

INVITATION:

Cut flame shapes from red art board, add streaks of gold glitter and inscribe the following birthday message using a gold pen. Or, purchase bright red invitations.

KATHY
is
4 0
and
RED HOT

Join us for a
"Flamin' Forties"
Birthday Frolic !!

Please wear red and honor Kathy with a "Red Hot" gift.

Date: Time:

Place:

MOOD SET:

Give your guests a rousing red welcome. Choose one or more of the following: a metallic red bow tied to your front doormat, planters filled with red geraniums, red netting draped across the doorway, or a festive banner announcing the "Flamin' Forties Frolic."

Select a favorite cut glass or other appropriate vase of a size suitable for an arrangement of long-stemmed flowers. Red gladiolus, bird-of-paradise or red roses are possibilities. Spray paint a few smooth, graceful tree branches with gold metallic paint to add just the right spark to this simple yet dramatic floral arrangement.

To ignite white linen napkins, tie with strips of red tulle and gold metallic ribbon. Additional strips of red tulle and gold ribbon can be swirled gracefully across a white linen cloth or draped from the chandelier. The flicker of votive candles nestled amid the ribbons and tulle are also effective. For placecards, cut red tulle into 5-inch squares, fill with your favorite red hot candy, bring the corners to the center, and secure using narrow red and gold ribbons. Attach a small white card with guest's name inscribed in gold ink. A light dusting of gold glitter adds a finishing touch to the entire tablescape.

ENTERTAINMENT:

Obviously, opening red-hot birthday gifts will be entertainment in itself, but here is an amusing "warm up" you may incorporate. Set a short time limit. Provide each guest with paper and a pen and instruct them to list phrases dealing with "red" or "hot". The winner is assured a "steamy" prize. Examples:

"Red as a beet"
"Hot as a pistol"
"Red rover, red rover"
"Hot Chihuahua"

Should one of your guests need a gift idea, you might suggest a sultry romance novel, red lingerie, gift certificate for a manicure, pedicure or massage.

MENU:
The following menu is appropriate for a ladies' luncheon:

Bloody Marys*
or
Red Wine
Cheese Wafers
Quicky Quiche*
Red Hot Salad*
Fresh Steamed Asparagus with Red Pepper Rings
Cherries Jubilee
or
Your Favorite Birthday Cake Topped with Sparklers

The Italian menu suggested for the Singing Waiter Party is appropriate when observing a gentleman's birthday.

<u>MEMENTO</u>:
Purchase or make a small, appropriately red gift for each guest, wrap in red and gold colors and use at each place setting.

Gone With The Wind

Close your eyes, Miss Scarlett, and Rhett might appear at your party. This lavish 40th birthday party is a superb way to celebrate the passing of youth, "Gone with the Wind". You will be speaking with a delicious Southern drawl for days!

INVITATION:

Include a silk magnolia blossom or small Confederate flag with each copy of the following invitation. Mail in a mailing tube, or deliver by hand.

Let's celebrate Mike's 40 years
With magnolias, juleps & southern cheers.
We'll capture days of long ago
When "Tara" stood form proudly so.
Come in costume, a belle or gent
To celebrate Mike's youth well spent.
On May 3, Come be his friend
'Cause his young existence is...
Gone With The Wind
May 3   8:00 P.M.   404 Rockbrook
The Elliston Plantation

MOOD SET:

Turn your back lawn into a picturesque plantation. Achieve the desired effect by attaching clusters of magnolia leaves and blossoms to railings, porches or decks with wide white ribbon bows. A grapevine wreath adorned with more magnolia leaves, blossoms, and English ivy is sure to add a special touch. Display Confederate flags, lanterns, cotton and hay bales, old farm tools, watermelons and cotton or feed sacks.

Use hurricane lawn lamps to illuminate a pathway to canopied buffet tables, where an elaborate floral design of red, white and blue continues the Confederate theme.

Consider stringing miniature white lights in trees, or across awnings and porches to help light your Southern sky.

Use individual baskets lined with red and blue tissue paper to serve an authentic Southern supper for each gent and belle. Lawn furniture and quilts provide seating.

A flat bed wagon stacked with hay bales can provide service for beverages. Offer lemonade and minted tea in mason jars. Ice beverages in a nearby wheelbarrow. The heartier Southern soul can find stiff libations and good cigars at the adjacent ''gentlemen's table.''

ENTERTAINMENT:

This generous helping of Southern ambiance is complemented with a selection of background music: *Dixie, Old Man River,* songs from *Showboat, Porgy and*

112

Bess, Cotton Fields, and other Dixieland tunes. Of course, a professional Dixieland band would be superb.

Your guests' Southern costumes will provide entertainment and wonderful topics of conversation for everyone.

MENU:

Country Smoked Sliced Ham
on Split Rolls
Black-eyed Peas
Dill Pickle Spears
Best Ever Pralines*

Be sure and furnish napkins and appropriate silverware for each basket.

MEMENTO:
Hire a professional photographer to take plenty of candid shots throughout the evening. Mail a copy of a special picture to your guests.

Each Southern belle might receive a small hand fan to use on warm southern evenings; the gentlemen, cigars or a Confederate flag lapel pin.

Something Old Something New

Honor a bride with an intimate gathering of family and friends. This luncheon will seem so special as each guest brings "Something Old, and Something New" for the bride. Perhaps an old family photo in a lovely new frame, a pretty guest towel trimmed in antique lace, or even an heirloom sugar bowl filled with sugar-substitute packets. A blend of the past and present in a fairy tale setting will be an extraordinary affair.

INVITATION:
For a fanciful invitation, have a calligrapher copy the poem. Then duplicate the calligraphied message on ivory

Something old and something new,
That is what is asked of you.
A pair of gifts, an honored bride
Treasured memories will abide.
Come for Lunch this summer day,
Let's toast this bride a special way!

Honoring Miss Nancy Phillips
Saturday, June 10   12 Noon
at the home of
Mrs. John Jones, 1709 Timberlake Dr.

parchment paper. Tuck a lace handkerchief and some dried rose blossoms into the envelope. Trail a length of narrow ribbon in the bride's colors from the envelope before sealing.

MOOD SET:

Inside or outside, this party is steeped in sentiment and romance. Yards of white lace and tulle are important elements of this enchanting mood set. Begin your tablescape with crisp white linens swagged with tulle and tied with white satin bows. Then, a dried-flower tree will form a charming centerpiece for the dining table. Pour plaster of Paris into a flower pot. Center a dowel rod. After the plaster hardens, mount an 8-inch ball of foam. Cover the ball with assorted dried flowers. Distribute colors evenly. Some of the flowers can be wired to florist picks for insertion, while others may be glued directly to the foam ball. Use moss to fill in any empty spots.

Use ribbons for streamers and a top bow. Streamers may be anchored at each placesetting with a small memento for every guest.

Fold white linen napkins into an accordion fan. Secure the bottom of each fan with a bow of white lace. Insert a sweetheart rose under the lace bow just before your guests arrive. Swirl more lace and tulle on the table top.

In keeping with the "Something Old, Something New" theme, it would be appropriate to set the dining table with a selection of antique pieces: china, silver, or crystal. Intermingle new pieces with the old. This party is a wonderful opportunity to use many of those neglected heirlooms.

For a personal touch, place a violet, primrose, or pansy in a small bowl or sundae dish lined with a white doily. Then display one of these arrangements at every place setting. These could even serve as place card holders. Use more old-fashioned doilies to line salad and dessert plates, and as coasters for beverages.

Dried flowers can be used to create a sensational wreath for the front door. Reflect the bride's colors as you cover a foam or straw wreath.

ENTERTAINMENT:
Opening such wonderful gifts will be an experience all will enjoy, not just the bride. Be sure to share the stories and legacies of each gift.

MENU:
Summer Fruit with Mint Sauce
Curried Chicken Salad*
Poppy and Sesame Seed Knots*
Easy Chocolate Roll*
Almond Tea*

MEMENTO:
A pretty lace handkerchief would be a lovely momento for this party.

It's In The Bag

Food, flowers, frivolity,
everything for this delightful bridal shower is in the bag!

INVITATION:

A 6-x11-inch brown paper bag (white or other color lunch-type bags are often available) serves as your invitation, envelope, and gift wrap. With the smooth side of the bag facing up and open end of the bag facing toward you, write the following shower specifics on the top one third of each bag. (See page 120)

Following the natural creases of the bag, fold the top third down (the portion on which details were written-- see figures 1 & 2). The bottom one third folds up,

A shower is in the making for a bride-to-be:
Welcome Miss Nancy Adams as the honoree.
Tell her you care if she succeeds
By scripting on the card one of your recipes.
Giving Nancy a hint of your success
By bringing an ingredient to this address:
Mrs. Sam Davidson
700 Harris St.
Rockwall, Texas
Put your can or package or whatever it may be
In this brown bag, made especially for thee.
Tie it with care, using the ribbons inside,
The colors being those of the soon-to-be-bride.
Time, 7 Post Meridiem, will be here soon,
In the year of our Lord, come Saturday afternoon.
April 7

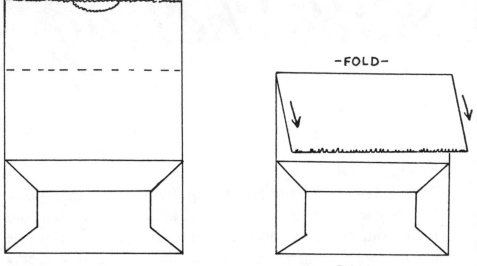

FIG. 1

-FOLD-

FIG. 2

-FOLD-

FIG. 3

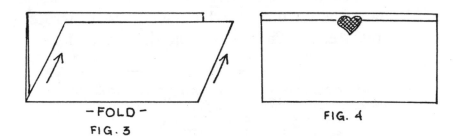

FIG. 4

M. BUCHANAN
1206 VALLEY DR.
CITY, TX 77277

Mrs. MIKE MILLS
26 PRINCE LN.
DALLAS, TX 75082

FIG. 5

120

covering the message (see figure 3). Staple, or use a decorative seal to hold the bag in place (see figure 4). Addresses should be inscribed on the center third. Affix a stamp, add return address, and this multi-purpose bag is ready to mail (see figure 5). Don't forget to enclose a recipe card and ribbons in each!

MOOD SET:
Prepare a whimsical welcome for the bride-to-be. Wrap your large outdoor planters or urns with brown paper. Gather at the top and tie with wide-ribboned bows, then

place on the front porch or entryway. On the door, hang a grapevine wreath decorated with small brown bags, ribbons, silk flowers, etc. to convey the "in the bag" theme. You might choose simply to open any size brown paper bag, secure it to the door, porch railing, courtyard gate, etc., and fill it with a bouquet of fresh or silk flowers. If the party takes place at night, line the driveway or sidewalk with luminaries.

The tablescape is extremely easy and appealing. Arrange fresh flowers which complement the bride's color selections in a vase or jar. Open some brown bags and position them on your table or buffet. Carefully lower the arrangements into the bags. Gather the bags around the top of the container and tie with colored ribbons. Prepare matching brown bag arrangements for use on guest tables, the mantel, the fireplace hearth, or other locations within your entertainment area.

ENTERTAINMENT:
An essential item to be presented to the honoree is a recipe file or box. Of course, it too, should be enclosed in a brown bag. The bride-to-be will delight in discovering the variety of recipes and ingredients brought by guests as she reveals the contents of each gift bag.

A lively means of involving all your guests is to plan an ingredient grab bag. Determine the size of each "grab bag team" based on your guest list (no more than four or five guests to a team). One grocery bag per team should be assembled in advance with a surprising combination of six or eight actual ingredients, a recipe card, and a pen. The challenge is to create a recipe using as many of the enclosed ingredients as possible. Each team is allowed to make one ingredient exchange with another willing team. The unique team recipes should be shared aloud, then presented along with the actual ingredients to the bride-to-be for her expanding recipe repertoire!

MENU:
Depending on the type of refreshments you desire, serving from bags may or may not be feasible. The following menu is suitable to service in bags using disposable containers (Chinese take-out buckets, small gift boxes or bags). Be sure to include necessary silverware and napkins.

Fruity Chicken Salad*
Carrot and Celery Sticks
Poppy and Sesame Seed Knots*
Marvelous Melt Aways*
Almond Tea*

MEMENTO:
Stencil bags, then bundle six or eight together for each guest to use as gift or lunch bags. Another option is to purchase or make a small gift for each shower guest and enclose it in a miniature paper bag. Use the mementoes at each place setting if the guests are to be seated, or fill a favorite basket with the mini-gift bags and incorporate with other decorations. Your guests will select mementoes from the basket as they depart.

Recipes

Contents

Appetizers and Beverages

ARTICHOKE SPREAD

1 (6-ounce) jar artichokes, well-drained
1 package Italian salad dressing mix
1 (16-ounce) package cream cheese

Soften cheese and combine with other ingredients. Refrigerate. Store in an air tight container.

CHEESE PUFFS

1 pound margarine
1 (5-ounce) jar Old English cheese spread
1 teaspoon tabasco
1 teaspoon onion powder
1 teaspoon beau monde powder
1½ teaspoons dill weed
1½ teaspoons worcestershire sauce
Dash cayenne pepper

Cream the margarine and cheese. Add tabasco, onion powder, beau monde, dill weed, worcestershire sauce and cayenne pepper. Use 2 large loaves of thin sliced bread. Remove all crusts. Stack 3 slices of bread. Spread bottom and middle slices with the cheese mixture. Place the third slice on top. Cut the sandwich into quarters and "ice" top and sides. Place the sandwiches onto a cookie sheet lined with waxed paper and freeze. When frozen, the cheese puffs may be removed from the cookie sheet and stored in freezer bags. To cook, place frozen puffs on foil covered cookie sheet and bake 15 to 20 minutes at 350°. Serve hot.

CHEESY APRICOT DIP

½ cup dried apricots
1 tablespoon sugar
1 (3-ounce) package cream cheese, cut into small pieces
½ cup sour cream
⅛ teaspoon nutmeg
Assorted fruit dippers: slices of apple and pear, pineapple
      chunks, strawberries, etc.

In a covered pan, simmer apricots in 1 cup of water for 15 minutes. Drain; reserve ¼ cup liquid. In a blender, combine apricots, liquid and sugar. Blend until smooth. Add cream cheese, sour cream and nutmeg. Blend again. Spoon into bowl, cover and chill. Makes 1⅓ cups.

DIGGER'S DIP

1 cup sour cream
1 cup lite salad dressing
2 teaspoons dill
2 teaspoons onion, finely grated
2 teaspoons lemon juice
½ teaspoon salt
1 teaspoon dry mustard

Combine the sour cream and salad dressing. Add remaining ingredients and mix well. Refrigerate for several hours before serving with carrot and celery sticks and zucchini, cucumber, and other vegetable slices.

FLOODWATER WAFERS

2 cups margarine, softened
1 pound sharp cheese, grated
4 cups flour
½ to 1 teaspoon cayenne pepper
½ cup pecans, finely chopped
Pecan halves

Blend the softened margarine and cheese in a large mixing bowl. Gradually add the flour, pepper and chopped pecans. Roll into small balls and refrigerate for at least 5 hours. Before baking, remove the balls from the refrigerator and leave them for about 10 minutes. Then place each ball on an ungreased cookie sheet and press a pecan half on top of each. Bake at 300° for 30 minutes or until lightly brown.

PINEAPPLE CHEESE BALL

2 (8-ounce) packages cream cheese, softened
1 (8-ounce) can crushed pineapple, drained
2 cups walnuts, chopped
¼ cup green pepper, finely chopped
2 tablespoons onion, finely chopped
1 tablespoon seasoned salt
1 (8-ounce) can pineapple rings
1 (6-ounce) jar maraschino cherries

Cream the cheese until smooth. Stir in the crushed pineapple, one cup of nuts, pepper, onion, and salt. Shape into a ball; coat with remaining cup of nuts. Cover tightly with plastic wrap and refrigerate overnight. Before serving, garnish with pineapple rings and cherries.

STUFFED MUSHROOMS

12 large fresh mushrooms
Melted margarine for brushing mushroom caps
2 tablespoons margarine
½ cup celery, finely chopped
½ cup green onions, finely chopped
½ cup green pepper, finely chopped
⅓ cup dry white wine
1 teaspoon worcestershire sauce
¼ cup bread crumbs
2 teaspoons Parmesan cheese, grated

Clean the mushrooms. Remove the stems, chop and set aside. Brush the mushroom caps with melted margarine. Melt the additional 2 tablespoons of margarine in a large skillet; when hot, add the chopped mushroom stems, celery, onion and green pepper. Sauté until tender. Add the white wine and worcestershire sauce and simmer for 5 minutes. Stir in the bread crumbs. Spoon the vegetable mixture into the mushroom caps. Place in a shallow baking dish, sprinkle with Parmesan cheese and bake for 18 to 20 minutes at 350°.

TOASTED PECANS

2 to 3 cups pecan halves
¼ cup margarine
Salt to taste

In a shallow pan or cookie sheet with rim, put a layer of pecans. Shake the pan gently to distribute the pecans evenly. Dot the pecans with margarine and place in a pre-heated oven at 325° for 5 minutes to melt the margarine. Remove and stir. Shake the pan each time you stir to level the pecans. Return to the oven for 10 minutes, then stir again. Continue this process until the pecans are toasted but not too brown. Some pecans toast faster than others. When the pecans are toasted, approximately 15 to 25 minutes, sprinkle with salt and stir. Let them cool in the pan. To assure crispness, do not place the pecans in a container until they have cooled.

ALMOND TEA

3 tablespoons instant tea
4 cups water
1½ cups sugar
1 (12-ounce) can frozen lemonade
2 quarts water (for lemonade)
3 teaspoons almond extract
3 teaspoons vanilla

Mix the instant tea with 2 cups water and set aside. Bring the remaining 2 cups of water to a boil, stir in the sugar, and set aside. Mix the lemonade with two quarts of water. Pour all together. Add the almond and vanilla extract, mixing well. Refrigerate. Delicious served hot or cold. Makes approximately 1 gallon.

BLOODY MARYS

3 ounces vegetable juice (such as V-8)
3 ounces Snappy Tom tomato juice
2 ounces vodka
Juice from a slice of lime or lemon
Salt to taste

Mix all ingredients thoroughly. Chill and serve.

MERRY BERRY JUICE

3 cups cranberry juice, chilled
1½ cups sparkling apple cider, chilled

Combine. Chill thoroughly. Garnish with lime slices.

SANGRIA

8 ounces orange juice
8 ounces pineapple juice
3 cups red wine
½ cup sugar

Mix all ingredients thoroughly. Chill and serve. Garnish with orange slices.

PURPLE COWS

Grape soda
Vanilla ice cream

Pour chilled grape soda into a tall glass. Fill to within 2 inches of the top. Add a scoop of vanilla ice cream. Serve with both a straw and a spoon.

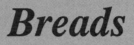

Breads

A TO ZUCCHINI BREAD AND SANDWICHES

3-4 medium-sized zucchini squash, grated to make 2 cups
2 cups sugar
1 cup vegetable oil
3 eggs
3 cups flour
1 teaspoon salt
1 teaspoon baking soda
1 teaspoon baking powder
3 tablespoons cinnamon
1 teaspoon vanilla
1 cup pecans, finely-chopped

In a large mixing bowl, combine the grated zucchini, sugar, oil and eggs. Mix well. Gradually add the flour, salt, soda, baking powder, cinnamon and vanilla. Continue to beat on low speed for 2 to 3 minutes. Fold in pecans. Pour into two greased-and-floured loaf pans. Bake at 325° until center springs to touch, about 55 minutes.
*To make A to Zucchini Sandwiches, slice the zucchini bread loaves. Spread with a filling of softened cream cheese (8 ounces) blended with crushed pineapple. Cut each sandwich into halves.

HERBED DINNER ROLLS

3 tablespoons grated Parmesan cheese
¼ teaspoon thyme
2 (8-ounce) packages refrigerated crescent dinner rolls
1 egg white, beaten
Poppy seeds

As you unroll the dough, do *not* separate into the triangle sections. Instead separate into 4 rectangles per can by pressing the perforated line. In a mixing bowl, combine the Parmesan cheese and thyme. Spread this cheese mixture over 6 of the rectangles. Stack 3 of those on each other then top with a plain rectangle. Repeat with the remaining 4 rectangles. Next cut each rectangle first lengthwise then crosswise. Cut each quarter into 2 triangles. Sprinkle with poppy seeds. Bake on a cookie sheet at 375° for 10-15 minutes.

HUSH-YOUR-MOUTH HUSHPUPPIES

4 cups cornmeal, stone ground preferable
1¾ cups flour
1½ tablespoons baking powder
Several green onions including tops, finely diced
1 egg
½ teaspoon pepper
½ teaspoon salt
2 cups beer

In a large mixing bowl, combine the cornmeal, flour, baking powder, pepper and salt. Blend well, then add all remaining ingredients. If the batter seems too stiff, add a bit more beer. Drop by teaspoon into very hot cooking oil (peanut oil works very well). Cook until golden brown. Serve while still hot.

LYNN'S SOURDOUGH BISCUITS

1 cup flour
1 teaspoon baking powder
½ teaspoon salt
¼ teaspoon baking soda
1 cup sourdough starter (recipe below)
⅓ cup oil

Mix all ingredients thoroughly. Turn out onto a floured surface. Knead lightly several times. Roll the dough or pat it out to ¾-inch thickness and cut. Bake at 400° until golden brown.

Sourdough Starter:

Mix and let stand 10 minutes:
½ cup warm water
1 (¼-ounce) package dry yeast

Add:
½ cup milk
1 cup flour
⅓ cup sugar

Let stand at room temperature 2-3 hours.   Then refrigerate 24 hours.
To feed the starter add:
1 cup flour
¼-⅓ cup sugar
1 cup milk

Feed the starter once before using it. When using a cup of the starter for a recipe, feed it again to maintain your starter. To store sourdough starter, make sure the lid on the bowl is left ajar so it can "breathe". Stir every few days. The starter will keep almost indefinitely.

POPPY AND SESAME SEED KNOTS

1 (11-ounce) package refrigerator breadsticks
2 tablespoons margarine, melted
⅓ teaspoon sesame seeds
⅓ teaspoon poppy seeds

Preheat oven to 350°. Separate breadstick dough. Loosely tie each strip into a knot and place about 1 inch apart on a cookie sheet. Brush each knot lightly with melted margarine. Sprinkle with seeds. Bake 15 minutes or until golden brown.

PUMPKIN BREAD

3 cups sugar
4 eggs
1 cup oil
⅔ cup water
1 (1-pound) can pumpkin
3½ cups flour
2 teaspoons baking soda
1½ teaspoons cinnamon
1 teaspoon nutmeg
1½ teaspoons salt
2 cups pecans, chopped

Use mixer to combine sugar, eggs, oil, water and pumpkin. Add the flour, soda, cinnamon, nutmeg and salt. Beat for 4 to 5 minutes or until smooth. Stir in the pecans. Pour into 2 greased loaf pans and bake at 350° for 55 minutes.

Desserts

APPLE SPICE CAKE

2 cups sugar
1¼ cups vegetable oil
2 eggs
1 teaspoon vanilla
3 cups flour
1 teaspoon baking soda
1 teaspoon cinnamon
½ teaspoon salt
1 cup pecans, chopped
3 cups apples, peeled and chopped

Combine the sugar, oil, eggs and vanilla in a large mixing bowl. Gradually add the flour, soda, cinnamon, and salt. Blend well. Fold in the apples and pecans. Pour into a greased-and-floured 9×13-inch cake pan. Bake 350° for 35 minutes. Serve warm with a dollop of whipped cream.

APRICOT SQUARES

2 cups sifted flour
1 cup sugar
¼ teaspoon cream of tartar
1 cup margarine
5 egg yolks
1 (18-ounce) jar apricot preserves

Sift the flour, sugar and cream of tartar; then cut in the margarine as for a pie crust. Add the egg yolks and mix well. Pat about ¾ of the dough into a 15×10-inch cookie sheet making the sides a little higher than the center. Spread the preserves over the top. Roll remaining dough on well-floured board, adding flour as needed. Cut into strips and arrange in lattice across the top of the preserves. Bake at 375° until brown, approximately 30 to 35 minutes. Cool before slicing into squares.

BEST EVER PRALINES

½ cup brown sugar
1½ cups sugar
½ cup evaporated milk
3 tablespoons light corn syrup
1½ cups miniature marshmallows
1 tablespoon margarine
1 teaspoon vanilla
2½ cups pecans, chopped

In a medium-sized sauce pan, mix both sugars with the milk and corn syrup. Place over medium heat and stir often. Heat until the mixture reaches 240° F, the soft-boil stage. Remove from the heat and rapidly beat the mixture. Then add the marshmallows, margarine and vanilla. Beat again. Add the pecans and continue to beat until the mixture begins to cool and lose its gloss. Quickly drop by teaspoon onto wax paper. If the praline mixture in the pan begins to harden, simply add a few drops of water, stir and continue.

BLUEBERRY CHEESECAKE

Crust:
16 graham crackers
¼ cup sugar
½ cup margarine

For crust, mix the graham crackers, sugar and margarine. Press into a 7×12-inch glass casserole. Do not bake.

Filling:
1 (16-ounce) package cream cheese, softened
1 cup sugar
2 eggs
1 teaspoon vanilla

For the filling, beat the softened cream cheese, sugar, eggs and vanilla. Pour into the crust and bake at 350° for 20 minutes.

Topping:
1 (16-ounce) can blueberries, waterpacked
2½ tablespoons cornstarch
½ cup sugar
2 tablespoons lemon juice

For the topping, thicken the juice from the blueberries with the cornstarch, sugar and lemon juice. Cook over medium heat until thickened. Let the mixture cool before adding the well-drained blueberries. Spread this over the cooled cheesecake. Refrigerate until ready to serve. Slice into squares and top with whipped cream. This can be prepared 1 to 2 days in advance.

CARAMEL NUT BROWNIES

1 (14-ounce) package caramels
⅔ cup evaporated milk
1 German chocolate cake mix
¾ cup melted margarine
1 cup chocolate chips
1 cup pecans, chopped

Melt caramels with ⅓ cup of milk in double boiler. In a mixing bowl, combine cake mix with melted margarine and remaining milk. Spread ½ cake mixture into greased 9×13-inch pan. Bake 4-5 minutes at 350°. Remove from oven. Sprinkle with chocolate chips and pecan pieces. Drizzle with melted caramels and cover with remaining cake batter. Bake 10 minutes more at 350°.

CHOCOLATE AMARETTO CHEESECAKE

Crumb Crust:
1 (8½-ounce) package chocolate wafers, crushed
¼ cup sugar
1 teaspoon cinnamon
6 tablespoons margarine
2 tablespoons amaretto

Mix ingredients together and press evenly in bottom and up sides of 10-inch springform pan. Bake at 400° for 10 minutes. Remove from oven and let cool.

Filling:
5 (8-ounce) packages cream cheese, softened
1 (6-ounce) package semi-sweet chocolate chips, melted
       and cooled
1¾ cups sugar
3 tablespoons flour
1½ teaspoons lemon juice
¼ teaspoon vanilla
Dash of salt
5 eggs
2 egg yolks
¼ cup whipping cream
¼ cup amaretto

In large mixing bowl, beat cream cheese until smooth. Add sugar, melted chocolate, flour, lemon juice, vanilla and salt. Beat until well blended, scraping sides occasionally. Beat in the eggs and egg yolks, one at a time, until light and fluffy. Beat in cream and then amaretto. Pour into prepared pan. Let stand 10 minutes at room temperature. Bake 10 minutes at 400°. Reduce heat to 250° but do not open the oven door. Bake 1 hour and 5 minutes more. Remove from oven. Immediately, run spatula or knife around edge of cake to loosen from sides of pan. This helps prevent cake from cracking. Cool in pan or wire rack 1 hour, then cover and refrigerate at least 4 hours. May be topped with additional whipped cream and chocolate shavings.

CHOCOLATE CHIP COOKIES
TO CHEER FOR

2 cups margarine, softened
2 cups sugar
2 cups brown sugar
5 eggs
2 teaspoons vanilla
4 cups flour
5 cups quick oatmeal
1½ teaspoons salt
2 teaspoons baking soda
2 teaspoons baking powder
24 ounces chocolate chips
16 ounces chocolate candy bar, grated
2-3 cups pecans, chopped

In a large mixing bowl, blend the margarine, sugars, vanilla and eggs. In a blender or processor, grind the oats to a powdery stage. Then, gradually add the flour and oatmeal to the sugar mixture. Next, add the salt soda, baking powder, chocolate and pecans. Blend well. Refrigerate for at least 1 hour. Roll the dough into 1-inch balls and bake on an ungreased cookie sheet at 350° until lightly brown. Do not overbake.

EASY CHOCOLATE ROLL

6 eggs, room-temperature and separated
½ cup sugar
4 tablespoons cocoa
1 tablespoon flour

Line a jelly roll pan with wax paper. Put aside.

Beat the egg yolks until a frothy-lemon color. Add sugar, cocoa and flour. Blend well. In a separate mixing bowl, beat the egg whites until stiff. Gently fold the egg whites into the first mixture. Spread the batter in the lined jelly roll pan. Bake at 350° for about 30 minutes or until springs back to touch.

After the cake has cooled for 10 minutes, turn it upside-down onto a slightly damp towel. Pull back the paper and then gently roll the cake in the towel as a log shape. Place in the refrigerator for at least 30 minutes.

Filling:
½ pint whipping cream
⅓ cup sugar
¼ cup chocolate syrup

While cake is cooling, whip the whipping cream and sugar. Fold in the chocolate syrup until well-blended. Unroll the cake; spread with the whipped cream mixture then roll the cake again. Refrigerate until ready to serve. Dust with powdered sugar before slicing.

GILDED ALMOND DELIGHTS

½ cup margarine
¼ cup sugar
3 tablespoons cocoa
2 teaspoons vanilla
1 egg
1 cup almonds, toasted and slivered
1¾ cups vanilla wafer crumbs
Cream Filling (recipe below)
1 (12-ounce) package chocolate chips

In a medium pan, combine first 5 ingredients and cook over low heat, stirring constantly, until the mixture thickens. Remove from heat, add almonds, vanilla wafer crumbs. Stir well. Press into ungreased 9×13-inch pan, cover and chill. Prepare the Cream Filling and spread it over almond mixture; cover and chill. Cut into squares. Remove from pan and place on wax paper. Set aside. Place chocolate in a heavy-duty plastic bag. Submerge into hot water until chocolate melts. Cut a small hole in the corner of the bag. Drizzle the chocolate over the Cream Filling.

Cream Filling:
⅓ cup margarine, softened
1 egg
½ teaspoon vanilla
2½ to 3 cups powdered sugar

Cream margarine, beating at a high speed with an electric mixer. Add egg and vanilla, mix well. Slowly add sugar, mixing until smooth.

MARINATED STRAWBERRIES IN RUM

1 pint fresh strawberries
¼ cup light rum
⅓ cup sour cream
½ cup powdered sugar
3 tablespoons coconut, toasted

Hull strawberries and slice. In a mixing bowl, combine berries and rum and set aside for 15 minutes. In another bowl, combine sour cream and powdered sugar. To serve, spoon berries into dessert dishes and top with cream mixture. Garnish with toasted coconut.

MARVELOUS MELT AWAYS

1 (1-pound) box light brown sugar
⅔ cup shortening, melted
2¾ cups flour
2½ teaspoons baking powder
½ teaspoon salt
3 eggs, beaten
1 cup pecans, chopped
1 (12-ounce) package chocolate chips

In a mixing bowl, combine the sugar with the melted shortening; cool. Add flour, baking powder, salt, and eggs. Mix well. Fold in pecans and chocolate chips. Pour into a greased-and-floured 9×13-inch casserole. Bake at 300° for 25 minutes or until golden. Cut into squares.

MISSISSIPPI MUD PIE

1½ cups sugar
3 eggs
½ cup margarine, melted
1 teaspoon vanilla
5 tablespoons cocoa, heaping
1 cup pecans, chopped

Combine all ingredients except for pecans. Mix well. Add pecans. Pour into an unbaked pie shell. Bake at 350° until set, approximately 40 minutes. Serve with a scoop of ice cream or a dollop of whipped cream.

MOMENTOUS BON-BONS

2 (one-pound) boxes powdered sugar
1 (14-ounce) can sweetened condensed milk
½ cup margarine, melted
1½ teaspoons vanilla
1 cup chopped nuts
1 (12-ounce) package chocolate chips
¼ pound parafin

Combine first 5 ingredients in a large mixing bowl. Blend well. Roll into ½-inch balls and refrigerate for at least 3 hours. In a double boiler, melt the chocolate chips and parafin and blend. Using a toothpick, dip each ball in the chocolate mixture and place on wax paper. This dipping process must be quick since the chocolate will harden quickly.

MOTHER'S BROWN SUGAR COOKIES

1 cup shortening
2 cups brown sugar
2 eggs
3½ cups flour
1 teaspoon vanilla
1 cup pecans, chopped

In a mixing bowl, cream the shortening and brown sugar. Add the eggs, flour and vanilla, mixing well. Fold in the pecans. Divide the dough into two equal amounts. Place each portion on a sheet of wax paper, shaping into a long log. Wrap each log in the wax paper. Chill for several hours or overnight. Slice the dough into ¼-inch sections; place on an ungreased cookie sheet and bake at 350° for approximately 10 to 12 minutes or until browned.

Note:
The dough will keep well in the refrigerator.

PUMPKIN ROLL

3 eggs
1 cup sugar
⅔ cup pumpkin
1 teaspoon lemon juice
¾ cup flour
½ teaspoon salt
1 teaspoon baking powder
2 teaspoons cinnamon
1 teaspoon ginger
½ teaspoon nutmeg
1 cup pecans, chopped

Beat the eggs on high speed for 5 minutes. Add the sugar, pumpkin and lemon juice. Add the dry ingredients and beat on lower speed until smooth. Spread the batter in a jelly roll pan (11×16-inch) lined with wax paper. Sprinkle with pecans. Bake at 375° for 15 minutes. Immediately remove from the pan. Invert onto a dish towel. Roll with the wax paper and let cool. Then unroll, remove paper, spread with filling, and roll again. Cover and refrigerate for at least 45 minutes. Slice to serve.

Filling:
1 cup powdered sugar
1 (8-ounce) package cream cheese, softened
4 tablespoons margarine, softened
1 teaspoon vanilla

Combine all ingredients beating until smooth. Spread as instructed.

RASPBERRY MOUSSE

5 egg whites
2 cups whipping cream
¼ cup powdered sugar
1 teaspoon vanilla
1 teaspoon blackberry brandy
1 tablespoon raspberry extract
1 pint fresh raspberries*

In a small mixing bowl, beat the egg whites until soft
stiff peaks form. Set aside. In a separate bowl, beat
the whipping cream until stiff, then add powdered
sugar. Fold the beaten egg whites and whipped cream
together. Add vanilla, blackberry brandy and
raspberry extract to the egg white/cream mixture.
Gently fold the fresh raspberries into the mixture.
Spoon into dessert glasses and refrigerate for 2 to 4
hours. Serves 4 to 6 depending on the size dessert
glasses used.

*If fresh raspberries are not available, a 10-ounce
package of frozen raspberries may be substituted.
Thaw and drain the berries before folding into the
flavored mix.

RASPBERRY PARFAIT

2 (3-ounce) packages of raspberry gelatin
1½ cups water
1 (8-ounce) carton sour cream
1 pint raspberry sherbet
30 ounces frozen raspberries with juice, thawed
2 cups whipping cream
½ cup powdered sugar
Mint sprigs

Boil the water and dissolve the gelatin in it. Add the sour cream and sherbet. Stir until melted in the mixture. Add the raspberries and juice. Blend well. Pour into 8 to 10 parfait or wine glasses. Cover each with plastic wrap then chill for several hours.
Before serving, whip the cream with the powdered sugar. Top each parfait with a dollop of whipping cream and a sprig of fresh mint.

SCRUMPTIOUS SAND TARTS

1 cup margarine
4 tablespoons powdered sugar, sifted
2 cups flour, sifted
1 teaspoon baking powder
1 cup pecans, finely chopped
1 teaspoon vanilla

Cream the margarine and powdered sugar. Sift together the flour and baking powder. Add the pecans and vanilla and mix thoroughly.

Shape dough into 2-inch crescent shapes and place on ungreased baking sheet. Bake at 350° for 10 to 12 minutes. Dust with powdered sugar while warm.

TEA PARTY TEA CAKES

1¾ cups flour
1 teaspoon baking powder
½ teaspoon baking soda
¼ teaspoon salt
½ cup margarine, softened
¾ cup sugar
1 egg
½ cup milk
Juice of 1 lemon, strained

In one mixing bowl, combine the flour, baking powder, baking soda, and salt. Set aside. In a larger bowl, combine the margarine and sugar. Blend well. Add the egg, milk, and 3 tablespoons of lemon juice. Blend again. Gradually add the dry ingredients from the first bowl. Mix well. Refrigerate for 1 hour then drop by teaspoon onto an ungreased cookie sheet. Bake at 350° until lightly golden. Remove and cool. Brush any remaining lemon juice on top, then sprinkle with sugar.

Meats and Main Dishes

ALASKAN KING SALMON
with Raspberry-Honey Sauce

6 (6-ounce) medallions of salmon
½ teaspoon salt
6 pieces of fresh dill
¼ teaspoon dried thyme
½ cup lemon juice
4 tablespoons brown sugar
3 tablespoons margarine, melted
2 cups honey

Rub salmon lightly with salt, lemon juice and herbs. Then coat salmon with a mixture of margarine, brown sugar and honey. Finally, broil salmon slowly until it flakes with a fork.

See Raspberry-Honey Sauce p. 181.

CAMPFIRE SKILLET DINNER

1 large onion, chopped
1 tablespoon margarine
1 pound ground beef, lean
1 (10-ounce) can tomatoes
1 large green pepper, chopped
1 (16-ounce) can corn niblets, drained
1 (16-ounce) can kidney beans, drained
1½ teaspoons salt
½ teaspoon pepper
1 tablespoon chili powder
½ teaspoon garlic powder
1 (8½-ounce) package cornmeal muffin mix

In a large cast iron skillet, sauté the onion in the margarine. Add the ground beef, stirring until crumbled and browned. Drain excess fat. Add the tomatoes, cover and simmer for 20 minutes. Mix in the green pepper, corn, beans, salt, pepper, chili powder and garlic powder; blend thoroughly. Prepare the muffin mix according to package directions. Drop this mixture by spoonfuls across the top of the casserole then bake for 30 to 40 minutes at 400°.

CHICKEN LOAF
with Mushroom Sauce

1 hen, cooked, deboned and diced; save broth
2 cups bread crumbs
1 cup cooked rice
1½ teaspoons salt
4 beaten eggs
⅛ cup diced pimento
3 cups milk or chicken broth (half of each is preferred)

Mix all ingredients adding the eggs last. Place in a
9×13-inch casserole and bake for 1 hour at 325°.
Slice into squares and top with mushroom sauce.

See Mushroom Sauce p. 180.

CORNISH HENS

8 cornish hens
12 large cloves of garlic, peeled and minced
4 teaspoons oregano
Salt and pepper to taste
1 cup red wine vinegar
½ cup oil
1 cup pitted prunes
1 cup dried apricots
1 cup pitted green olives
7 bay leaves
1 cup brown sugar
1 cup dry white wine
3 tablespoons parsley, chopped

Clean the hens and pat dry. Arrange the hens in a shallow baking pan. Combine the garlic, oregano, salt and pepper, vinegar, oil, prunes, apricots, olives and bay leaves. Spoon this mixture over the hens. Cover and refrigerate overnight. When ready to bake, preheat the oven to 350°. Again, spoon the prune/apricot mixture over the hens. Sprinkle evenly with brown sugar and parsely then pour the wine into the baking pan. Bake for 1 to 1½ hours, basting often.

LAYERED CHICKEN ENCHILADA CASSEROLE

2 pounds of deboned chicken breasts, cooked and
       shredded
1 medium onion, diced
1 bell pepper, green or gold, diced
1 (10-ounce) can enchilada sauce
2 (10½-ounce) cans cream of chicken soup
1 (4-ounce) can of chopped green chilies
1 pound cheddar cheese, grated
12 corn tortillas, softened in chicken broth

Sauté the onion and bell pepper in a small amount of
oil. In a large mixing bowl, combine the enchilada
sauce, chicken soup and green chilies.
Use a non-stick spray to coat a 9×13-inch casserole.
Cover the bottom of the dish with a layer of corn
tortillas. Add a layer of shredded chicken then pour ½
of the sauce mixture on top. Add a layer of cheese.
Repeat the layers: tortillas, chicken, sauce, and
cheese. Bake at 350° until bubbly, about 30 minutes.

LUSTY LASAGNA

1 pound ground chuck
1 small onion, diced
1 (28-ounce) can tomatoes
1 (12-ounce) can tomato paste
1 tablespoon sugar
1½ teaspoons salt
½ teaspoon oregano
½ teaspoon thyme
½ teaspoon red pepper
¼ teaspoon garlic salt
1 bay leaf
1 (16-ounce) package lasagna noodles
2 eggs
15 ounces ricotta cheese
16 ounces mozzarella cheese, grated

Over medium heat, cook the beef and onion until well browned, stirring often. Drain excess fat. Add the tomatoes and tomato paste, sugar, salt, oregano, thyme, pepper, garlic salt and bay leaf. Heat to boiling; stir to break up the tomatoes. Reduce to low heat and simmer for 30 minutes. Discard the bay leaf and spoon off any fat that accumulates. Prepare noodles and drain. In a 13×9-inch baking dish, arrange ½ of the noodles. Combine eggs and ricotta. Spoon ½ of this mixture over the noodles; sprinkle with ½ of mozzarella and ½ of sauce. Repeat. Bake at 375° for 45 minutes. Remove from the heat and let stand for 10 minutes before serving. Serves 8.

MEDITERRANEAN CHICKEN

8 chicken breasts; skinned, deboned, and dusted in
        flour
½ cup margarine
1 cup water
¾ cup chili sauce
5 tablespoons horseradish
½ cup ketchup
4 tablespoons worcestershire sauce
2 tablespoons lemon juice

In a large skillet, melt the margarine. Then brown the
chicken breasts in the melted margarine. Remove the
skillet from the heat. Combine the water, chili sauce,
horseradish, ketchup, worcestershire sauce and lemon
juice. Pour this mixture over the chicken and simmer.
As chicken cooks, add more water if needed. Cook
until tender, 35-40 minutes. Serve with the extra sauce
from the skillet.

QUICKY QUICHE

Pastry for a 9-inch pie

1 tablespoon poppy seeds
1⅓ cups coarsely shredded Swiss cheese
⅔ cup bacon, chopped, fried crisply and drained
⅓ cup sliced green onion
4 eggs, beaten
1⅓ cups sour cream
1 teaspoon salt
1 teaspoon worcestershire sauce

Combine first 5 ingredients. Add remaining ingredients and pour into pie crust. Bake about 45 to 50 minutes at 350°. Cool 5 minutes before serving.

SAFARI STEW

1 (12-ounce) box frozen okra
1 (12-ounce) box frozen green peas
1 (12-ounce) box frozen corn
2 potatoes, diced
1½ onions, diced
1½ pounds lean stew meat
1 (10-ounce) can Rotel tomatoes
1 (10-ounce) can stewed tomatoes
2 (8-ounce) cans tomato sauce
1 cup water
2 cloves garlic, minced

Brown the stew meat in a small amount of oil. Add remaining ingredients and cook slowly until vegetables are done and consistency thick.

SESAME CHICKEN
with Red Plum Sauce

6 whole chicken breasts, deboned
1½ cups buttermilk
2 tablespoons lemon juice
2 tablespoons worcestershire sauce
1 teaspoon paprika
2 cloves garlic, minced
4 cups soft bread crumbs, blended to a fine consistency
½ cup sesame seeds
¼ cup margarine, melted
¼ cup shortening, melted

Combine buttermilk, lemon juice, worcestershire sauce, paprika, and garlic. Dip the chicken breasts in this mixture, coating completely. Cover and refrigerate overnight. Drain thoroughly. Combine fine bread crumbs and sesame seeds. Toss to coat the chicken breasts. Place in a greased shallow baking dish. Combine the margarine and shortening and lightly brush on each breast. Bake for 35 to 40 minutes at 350°.

See: Red Plum Sauce p. 181.

Soups and Sauces

BLACK BEAN SOUP

2 cups black (turtle) beans
Water
½ onion, diced
2 cloves garlic, diced
2 tablespoons vegetable oil
1 chicken bouillon cube
Salt to taste

In a saucepan, cover the beans with water. Bring to a rapid boil, reduce heat and simmer. Next, sauté onion and garlic in the oil until lightly brown. Combine this with the beans and continue to simmer over low heat for several hours until beans are tender. Remove any foam as it accumulates. Add the chicken bouillon cube and salt to taste.

CORN CHOWDER

1 pound onions, diced
1 stick margarine
2 pounds frozen cut corn
1 quart chicken stock
1 quart half-and-half
½ cup bacon, crisp and diced
Salt and pepper to taste

Sauté onions in margarine until they are transparent. Add the corn and the chicken stock. Cook until the corn is tender. Add the half-and-half and chopped bacon. Season to taste with salt and pepper. Heat thoroughly but do not boil.

VEGETABLE CHEESE SOUP

4 tablespoons margarine, melted
½ cup onion, diced
½ cup celery, chopped
½ cup carrots, diced
2½ cups chicken broth, low-salt
1¼ cups potatoes, diced
3¼ cups American cheese, grated

In a large sauce pan, melt the margarine and add the onion, celery, and carrots. Cook on moderate heat until onions become transparent. Add the chicken broth and potatoes. Simmer for 20 minutes and then add the grated cheese. Blend and serve immediately.

CURRY SAUCE

3 or 4 onions, whole
⅔ pound brown sugar
1 (14-ounce) bottle ketchup
1 (14-ounce) bottle vinegar
½ tablespoon curry powder
1 teaspoon salt
½ teaspoon red pepper

Boil the onions for 5 minutes, then drain and chop. Mix all remaining ingredients and simmer for 30 minutes over low heat.

Slice a fully-cooked ham into ¼-inch slices. Layer the ham slices and sauce in a baking dish. Bake at 350° for 30 minutes.

HOT MUSTARD SAUCE

1 cup malt vinegar
3 small tins dry mustard
2 egg yolks
1 cup sugar

Mix the malt vinegar and dry mustard. Store in airtight container and let stand overnight. Mix the eggs and sugar, add to the mustard/vinegar mixture and beat with an electric mixer for one minute on medium speed. Put into double boiler and cook over medium heat for approximately 20 minutes, stirring constantly to remove any lumps. This will keep indefinitely in the refrigerator.

MUSHROOM SAUCE

¼ cup margarine
¼ cup flour
¼ cup milk
1 pint chicken broth
½ teaspoon lemon juice
½ cup mushrooms, chopped

Melt margarine and add flour, then milk. Mix well, then add broth and mushrooms, lemon juice and salt to taste. Stir constantly over medium heat until well-blended and hot.

RASPBERRY - HONEY SAUCE

1 pound fresh raspberries
1 pound powdered sugar
½ cup lime juice
2 cups honey
2 teaspoons cornstarch

Cook the raspberries, sugar, honey and lime juice until the mixture liquifies. Put through a strainer. Add cornstarch, and if desired, a jigger of cherry brandy, mixing thoroughly. To serve with salmon, pour a small amount of sauce onto each serving plate. Place a slice of prepared salmon on top of the sauce. Garnish with lemon wedges.

RED PLUM SAUCE

1½ cups red plum jam
1½ tablespoons prepared mustard
1½ tablespoons prepared horseradish
1½ teaspoons lemon juice

Combine all ingredients in a small pan; stir often while heating until warm.

Salads and Relishes

AVOCADO-SHRIMP SALAD

1 pound small shrimp, boiled, cleaned and deveined
2 medium avocados cut into 1-inch cubes
1 tablespoon onion, minced
⅓ cup celery, chopped
⅓ cup green pepper, chopped
½ teaspoon dried whole basil leaves
¼ teaspoon salt
2 tablespoons lemon juice
¼ cup salad dressing
¼ cup ketchup
Dash paprika
1 teaspoon lemon juice
Lettuce leaves
2 hard boiled eggs, sliced
Ripe olives
1 small tomato, quartered

Combine cooked shrimp and next 7 ingredients and set aside. Combine salad dressing, ketchup, paprika and 1 teaspoon lemon juice, mix well and set aside.

Place shrimp mixture onto lettuce leaves and pour dressing over each serving. Garnish with tomato wedge, ripe olives and boiled egg.

CURRIED CHICKEN SALAD

3 cups chicken-flavored rice, cooked and chilled
1½ teaspoons curry powder
2 tablespoons vegetable oil
1 medium onion, diced
1 pound chicken breasts, cooked, deboned and diced
1 cup celery, diced
1 bell pepper, diced
¾ cup lite salad dressing
1 (5-ounce) can water chestnuts, sliced

Combine the rice, curry powder, oil, and onion in a large bowl. Chill for one hour. Add chicken, celery, pepper, salad dressing and water chestnuts. Chill. Serve on a bed of lettuce.

FRESH SPINACH SALAD

Spinach, fresh, washed and torn into bite sizes
Mushrooms, washed and sliced
¾ cup olive oil
¼ cup tarragon vinegar
1 teaspoon garlic, minced
1 teaspoon onion, minced
1 teaspoon sugar
¼ teaspoon dry mustard
½ teaspoon celery salt
1 cup Feta cheese, crumbled
1 cup walnuts, toasted and chopped

Several hours before serving this salad, combine the oil, vinegar, garlic, onion, sugar, dry mustard and celery salt. Blend well and refrigerate. At serving time, toss the spinach, mushrooms, cheese and walnuts with the dressing and serve.

FRUITY CHICKEN SALAD

1 (15¼-ounce) can pineapple tidbits, reserve juice
4 cups chicken, cooked and diced
1 (11-ounce) can Mandarin oranges, drained
1 (8-ounce) can water chestnuts, drained and sliced
1 (2½-ounce) package almonds, sliced and toasted
1 cup celery, diced
1 cup seedless green grapes, halved
1½ cups mayonnaise
1 tablespoon soy sauce
1 tablespoon curry powder
1 (3-ounce) can chow mein noodles

Drain pineapple, reserving 2 tablespoons of juice.
Combine pineapple and next 6 ingredients. Mix
thoroughly. Combine 2 tablespoons pineapple juice
and remaining ingredients except noodles. Stir well
and add to chicken. Chill. Stir in noodles just before
serving.

RED HOT SALAD

1 cup red hot candy
2 cups water
2 (3-ounce) packages lemon gelatin
1 cup applesauce
¾ cup pecans, chopped

Combine red hots with water and cook over low heat
until boiling; stir often. Remove from heat, add
gelatin and stir until dissolved. Add applesauce and
stir well. Add pecans. Pour into 9×13-inch casserole
or into individual molds and refrigerate until set.

TEACHER'S PET PEAR SALAD

4 cups fresh pears, unpeeled and chopped
1 cup dates, chopped
½ cup celery, chopped
½ cup almonds, slivered
⅓ cup yogurt, unflavored
½ teaspoon cinnamon

Combine pears, dates, celery and almonds. Gently mix them. In a separate container blend the yogurt and cinnamon. Then pour this mixture over the salad. Toss and refrigerate briefly for 15 minutes.   Serve immediately.

VERMICELLI SALAD

1 (12-ounce) package vermicelli
Cook and rinse.

6 hard boiled eggs, diced
1 (6-ounce) jar pimento, diced
6 stalks celery, diced
1 bunch green onions, diced
1 tablespoon dried parsley
Salt and pepper to taste
1 green pepper, diced
1½ pounds shrimp, cooked, cleaned and deveined
1 pint mayonnaise
Juice of 2 lemons
Horseradish to taste
Red pepper sauce to taste

Mix all ingredients, adding the cooked shrimp last. Refrigerate.

WARM WINTER FRUIT SALAD

1 (16-ounce) can pineapple chunks
1 (16-ounce) can peaches
1 (16-ounce) can apricots
1 (16-ounce) can pears
⅓ cup margarine, melted
⅔ cup brown sugar
¼ teaspoon nutmeg
¼ teaspoon cinnamon

Drain all fruits and pour into a casserole dish.
Combine the remaining ingredients and sprinkle over
the fruit. Bake at 325° for 20 minutes, until bubbly.
Serve warm.

GREEN TOMATO RELISH

4 quarts green tomatoes, cut into bite-sizes
6 medium onions, diced
6 bell peppers, diced
3 cloves garlic, diced
5 cups sugar
3 cups vinegar
1½ teaspoons tumeric
1½ teaspoons celery seed
2 tablespoons mustard seed

Combine the tomatoes, onions, peppers, and garlic,
then cover with ⅓ cup salt and chill for 3 hours.

Bring the sugar, vinegar, tumeric, celery and mustard
seed to a boil. Add well-drained vegetables to the
boiling liquid and boil 5 minutes more. Seal in
sterilized canning jars.

TOMATO JACK

1 large, firm tomato, diced
1 large green pepper, diced
1 medium onion, diced
1 tablespoon sugar
Your favorite hot sauce

Combine the diced tomato, pepper, and onion in a
small bowl. Sprinkle with the sugar and pour
approximately ¼ to ⅓ cup of the hot sauce over all.
Mix thoroughly. You may add more hot sauce to coat
the vegetables. This should not be watery.
Refrigerate.

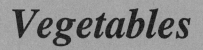

Vegetables

MOTHER'S BAKED BEANS

1 (16-ounce) can pork and beans
2 cups ketchup
4 tablespoons brown sugar
¼ teaspoon salt and pepper
3 tablespoons mustard
2 slices bacon, diced
2 tablespoons corn syrup
½ medium onion, diced

Combine all ingredients, pour into a casserole dish and bake at 375° for 35 to 45 minutes.

OKRA GUMBO

1 pound fresh okra
3 slices bacon, fried crisply and crumbled (save 2
        teaspoons bacon drippings)
1 large onion, diced
1 medium green pepper, diced
1 (16-ounce) can tomatoes
¼ teaspoon each of salt, pepper and garlic salt

Wash okra, remove top stem section. Pat dry. Cut into 1-inch pieces. In a large skillet, cook the okra in the reserved bacon drippings until lightly browned, add onion and pepper and cook until tender. Stir in tomatoes, salt, pepper and garlic salt. Cover and simmer for 20 minutes. Add bacon bits before serving.

PERKY PINEAPPLE

8 slices of white bread
½ cup milk
2 cups sugar
1 stick of margarine, softened
3 eggs, beaten
1 (5-ounce) can crushed pineapple, drained

Cut the crust from the bread slices. Cut into small cubes then soak them in the milk while you continue with the next steps. Cream the sugar with the softened margarine. Add the eggs and pineapple. Blend well. Then combine this mixture with the bread/milk. Blend again. Pour into a deep ungreased casserole dish and bake for 1 hour at 325°.

PICKLED BEETS

2 pounds fresh beets
6 cups sugar
2 cups vinegar

Thoroughly clean the beets, place in a large pan and cover with water, cooking until tender.

Drain the beets, slice into pieces and pack into sterilized canning jars.

Bring the sugar and vinegar to hard boil, pour over the beets and seal the jars.